CHEERLEADING FROM QUICKSAND

A Practical Path Out of Burnout and Back to Yourself

By Lyndi Zavy

This publication is designed to provide accurate and authoritative information in regard to the subject matter covered. It is sold with the understanding that neither the author nor the publisher is engaged in rendering legal, investment, accounting or other professional services. While the publisher and author have used their best efforts in preparing this book, they make no representations or warranties with respect to the accuracy or completeness of the contents of this book and specifically disclaim any implied warranties of merchantability or fitness for a particular purpose. No warranty may be created or extended by sales representatives or written sales materials. The advice and strategies contained herein may not be suitable for your situation. You should consult with a professional when appropriate. Neither the publisher nor the author shall be liable for any loss of profit or any other commercial damages, including but not limited to special, incidental, consequential, personal, or other damages.

Cover design by Jen Blair

First Edition 2026

For Woobie.

rivers 'til I reach you.

TABLE OF CONTENTS

INTRODUCTION

Slowly Sinking, Still Clapping

It all began in the bathroom. I know, it is a weird place to start, but unfortunately, we don't get to choose the site of our breakdowns.

Several years ago, on a cold January night, I went through the motions like I did most evenings. The after-school shuffle was followed by dinner and cleanup routines. I wasn't even aware of what I was doing: cooking, loading the dishwasher, scrubbing the stovetop, and wiping down the counters.

It was early January 2022, and I was becoming acquainted with grief. In November 2021, I lost my brother Jay to Chronic Lymphocytic Leukemia. We were told when he was diagnosed that it was survivable and that he would likely die "with it, not from it." We held onto that belief until his last day. I was living through the aftermath of losing a loved one, a loss that was swiftly followed by Thanksgiving and Christmas. Shockingly, I made it through both.

In the wake of his death, somehow, I trudged through Thanksgiving with friends and created Christmas magic for my kids when I was heartbroken. Did you know your kids notice if you don't move the Elf even when you're unsure how you're going to put one foot in front of the other?

I made it through the holidays only to enter the first year that my brother would never see. On New Year's Eve, I imagined writing a check with the new year. It's an archaic activity for sure, but almost instantly, I began sobbing, realizing that Jay would never enter the year 2022, nor would he ever date anything with the new year.

I sat on the floor of my closet (my favorite place to cry) and wept. That evening in my closet served as a warning sign of my upcoming breakdown, but I pulled myself together and trudged forward into the new year.

For the next few weeks, I kept working, parenting, leading, caring for my grieving parents, and managing my household. I didn't do any of it particularly well, but I did it.

That is, until that one seemingly typical January night. When I herded my children into the bathroom, I didn't think it would be a scene I'd remember for years to come, much less one I would write a book about.

I helped my then-three-year-old daughter into the bathtub while my eight-year-old son was around the corner in the shower. They happily splashed and played, as children often do immediately after acting like getting into the tub is the end of the world. But I got lost in my thoughts.

The sound of running water, the time of day, and the brief moment when no one was touching me or asking me for anything created a shift. The lavender scent of my daughter's bubble bath and the comfort of the routine surrounded me. I could simply *be.* As it turns out, my state of simply *being* was getting lost in my overwhelm, lost in the months that had just passed me by while I was just trying to get by.

I stood in the bathroom, staring at the gap between the tub and the shower. I was there, but I wasn't truly there.

In my mind, I was at Jay's funeral, listening to his friends and coworkers share heartfelt stories about him while I tried to keep my daughter entertained. I was fixing snacks in the kitchen of his beautiful home after the memorial service. I was flying back and forth from his house in California to my home in Oklahoma (six flights in three weeks, to be exact).

I was at work, listening to a comment my coworker made just days earlier: "Don't you think you've had enough time to grieve by now?" I was trying to remember the last time I had spent time with my husband, the man who loved me since my young-and-free twenties, the one now loving me through my darkest days. I was with my grieving parents, the ones going through what Lin-Manuel Miranda calls the *unimaginable* loss of losing a child, wondering if they had eaten food today.

As I stared at the wall in the bathroom, I felt like I was everywhere. And therefore, I was nowhere.

"Are you okay?"

I spun around and saw my husband, Brad. I don't know how long he had been standing there before he spoke. I hadn't realized he was there at all.

"No. I'm not okay," I heard myself say aloud.

It felt like everything hit me all at once: the grief, the hustle, the caretaking, and the love.

A deluge of sadness and pain rose to the surface. I'd been holding it back, but it poured out of me. I wept over the caretaking: for my precious parents, my sister, and my beautiful, wonderful children who didn't truly understand what we had all experienced. Honestly, none of us really did.

I wept over the hustle, a decades-long push of climbing higher and faster and leading people I cared for deeply.

But mostly, I wept for the love I felt for all these people, and the duty I felt to continue marching forward for them.

My family, my husband, and my kids.

My parents, my sister, and her family.

My brother and everything he left behind.

My brother's husband.

The people I led at work.

All these faces were on a loop in my mind, images flashing rapidly and never stopping. All the people I loved. All the people I wanted the best for. All the people I wanted to lift up and carry.

I was overwhelmed and didn't know where to turn. I felt more alone than I ever remember feeling. That's something no one tells you about grief: when your core family is also enduring the same grief, you can't turn to them in your time of need. They too are in their own valley of despair.

I'm not sure how long I cried, but eventually I said one of the bravest things I've ever said.

"I'm "I feel like I'm in a hole, and I don't know how to get out." Brad lifted my face to look at him and said, "We'll get you a ladder."

And we did, but first, we had to leave the bathroom. With Brad's help, we cleaned up the kids, then wrestled them into their pajamas and into bed. Maybe they even brushed their teeth, but I can't say for sure. (At least one of them had only baby teeth at that time, so I'm letting myself off the hook for that.)

Eventually, I crawled into my bed and slept enough to take the next steps the following day.

When I said I was in a hole, it was the best way I could describe it at the time. Looking back, I realize it was more than that. The hole was fighting me. Nothing could pull me out of it, and everything pushed me further down, into a place where no one could save me. It was more than a hole. I was in quicksand.

The quicksand didn't show up overnight. Rewind a few years before that moment, back to 2020. During the height of the COVID-19 pandemic, I was the accidental Chief Operating Officer (COO) at an infusion pharmacy.

How does someone become an accidental COO? Glad you asked. I first joined the team in 2017 in a Human Resources role that grew over the following years. As we approached the end of 2019, the company owners trusted me to run the organization alongside them, giving me a title I had never imagined possible.

Whether accidental or not, I was proud of this role, this title, and the responsibility to lead a team. What could possibly go wrong as a newly minted leader in the Year of Our Lord 2020? I had so much to look forward to, but … you know what 2020 brought, right?

Perhaps you have blocked it out, and who could blame you. For me, early 2020 meant daily changes to the recommendations for healthcare providers, workplaces, and individuals.

Let's check each employee's temperature every day. Actually, let's give them thermometers and let them self-report.

Masking doesn't help. Oh, wait, everyone should wear a mask. But only the right kind.

Our delivery manager talked to a patient, and it turns out the patient's wife has COVID. Should we test the driver? Yes. Actually, don't send him to the clinic. He was just a contact of a contact, and that's one step too far.

Was that a sniffle? Go home. Okay, come back. You're fine. We're short-staffed.

Pull your mask up over your nose, please. Yes, you still need to wear a mask.

I can't ask you to do that anymore, but please wear it in the common areas for our immune-compromised patients.

On and on it went, the whiplash of uncharted territory as a new and woefully unprepared leader faced a global health crisis.

By mid-2020, my team and I had gotten slightly better at managing the pandemic guidelines. It was by no means a picnic. On top of it all, a national organization was in the early stages of acquiring our company. I can't say that I recommend an acquisition during a global pandemic, but no one asked me. They just asked me to lead the organization through it.

On that note, may I share another thing I don't recommend when the world is in crisis? Moving. On February 29, 2020, on our first day of a five-day vacation with my family (our last one for a while, but we didn't know that at the time), our Realtor called and said, "You know how your house isn't on the market but you said you'd be willing to move? Full-price offer on the house if you can be out by March 25th." To which we said, "Sure, we can do that!"

A week after we returned home, our hometown NBA team canceled a game moments before tip-off due to COVID exposure. The world halted. Our contract, however, did not.

We moved without much help, before finding our next home, and into what we now affectionately call "the tiny house." Four humans, two dogs, one bathroom… and nowhere to escape. Even the grandparents' houses were closed to us. We were in the thick of it, but life kept moving forward.

One day, during the craziness of reviewing protocols during the day and touring houses in masks and disposable shoe covers at night, a co-worker asked, "How are you?"

My typical answer was "I'm livin' the dream!" regardless of what was going on around me. It usually felt true. But that day, I wasn't living any dreams, and I answered her honestly. I stopped in the hallway, lowered my shoulders away from my ears, and decided not to sugarcoat it.

"I'm cheerleading from quicksand."

I was taking care of others and lifting them up as a leader in the company, all while I felt like I was sinking.

When I looked around, my people were sinking, too. The people in my life, the ones I spent my days with both at home and at work, were all sinking alongside me. I know I wasn't alone in this. I am not sure anyone came out of the early 2020s unscathed, but I remember feeling like I wasn't fit to lead. My foundation was not solid enough to lift the people around me. I felt like I was cheerleading from quicksand.

In most institutions, organizational charts show the leaders at the top, but I don't think that's accurate. I see leaders as the base of a pyramid, holding others up just like the cheerleading pyramid. I was never a cheerleader in school, but I have watched '*Bring it On*' enough times to know that folks at the bottom serve as the foundation, using their core and leg strength to hold up the others. They rely on you to hold them steady. If your foundation is slippery, they are going to topple over comically right alongside you.

Stable or not, there I was, the leader at the base of both the organization and my home. Both roles I was happy to embrace. I was glad to hold them up. I like being a leader. I loved being a mom and wife. I enjoyed people relying on me. In fact, I liked it so much that at that moment, my obligation to lift them up was stronger than my need to pull myself out of the quicksand.

I knew my people also felt like they were sinking, and I felt a duty to lift them up more than I felt the need to make sure I didn't sink. What I didn't realize was that I couldn't actually hold them up if I was sinking. If I sank, I would take the whole team down with me. It took me a long time to come to that realization, years, to be exact.

That's why we started with that night in my bathroom.

That night was the first time I stopped moving long enough to realize that the quicksand was bringing me down, and I was sinking fast. I'm sure my kids were babbling in the bath or doing science experiments in the shower, but the only thing I could focus on was my own sinking.

I felt detached, like an observer. I couldn't find the joy that my kids found so naturally and easily. I felt a new, foreign disconnect between myself and the people I cared for at work, a detachment I couldn't put my finger on. The disassociation was gradual, like dimming the lights slowly until you can't see anything around you. It seemed like nothing I did made any difference, and I wasn't sure why I was still trying.

What I initially called a hole was actually sticky, messy quicksand. I realized that people depended on me, but I had become unreliable, certainly not by choice. I fought the quicksand as long as I possibly could, but it found me and pulled me into the muck. I entered the quicksand in the early days of the pandemic and kept sinking with the move, the acquisition, and then the immense grief.

The quicksand was my own personal puddle. Puddle sounds more harmless than it was, but like Pigpen's cloud of dirt, the quicksand followed me wherever I went. My natural tendency was to push harder to find my way out, to keep going even though I didn't have much left to give. I thought effort was the answer: more discipline, more grit, more endurance.

But truthfully, I knew better. I have always known that no change comes without self-awareness. I knew I couldn't solve a problem that I didn't fully understand, and I couldn't outwork this nameless thing. But I seemed to forget that in the darkness that is quicksand.

When I became aware that I was silently sinking, I could finally do something about it. I noticed the edge in my voice, the heaviness in my body, and the critical inner dialogue. That awareness provided me with language and a framework to help me respond differently.

Over time, I built routines and practices that helped me pause where I would normally power through. I learned to protect my energy before it was depleted and to make choices that aligned with my needs rather than with others' expectations of me. Life wasn't magically predictable, but it became more manageable. I recovered faster and I stopped disappearing into my responsibilities. I eventually climbed out of the quicksand and remained aware. When it inevitably came back—because life never stops—I could find my footing more quickly.

If the feelings that found me in the bathroom sound familiar to you, I hope this book helps you feel less alone. Have you been there? Are you sinking in quicksand? Maybe it didn't find you in the bathroom. Maybe it found you in a boardroom. Or maybe in a bar. Or in a bed that you just couldn't pull yourself out of one day. Maybe you're in it now. Quicksand goes by many names: Burnout. Exhaustion. Overwhelm.

Whatever you call it, I bet you can relate to that suffocating feeling. Maybe you are in it now. Wherever it found you, and however you found this book, I'm glad you're here. The title of this book is not the goal: I am not here to teach you how to keep cheerleading from quicksand. The goal is to get you onto solid ground, into a steady existence. I am here beside you with my pompoms, cheering you on as you find your way out of the quicksand.

Wait a second. Why quicksand?

In a 2010 Slate article, Daniel Engber interviewed fourth graders in New York City. He asked, "Are you afraid of quicksand?" The answer was a resounding, "No."[1]

Why would they be? Quicksand wasn't part of their lives. They didn't run into puddles of quicksand on their way to school.

But Engber suggested that children of his generation and the previous ones were completely terrified of quicksand. That would be my generation, the millennials, and even generations before me. We grew up watching Wesley save Buttercup from bogs of quicksand in *The Princess Bride* and watched Robin Williams sink into the attic-hardwood-floor-turned-deadly-pit in *Jumanji*. And the quicksand that could bring any 80s kid to tears: *The NeverEnding Story*.

Comedian John Mulaney said in a 2012 comedy bit, "I always thought quicksand was going to be a bigger problem than it turned out to be."[2]

Apparently, a lot of us did. According to Engber's data, quicksand scenes from my childhood made up 1% of movies. One in every hundred films from my childhood featured a swamp of quicksand. And that wasn't even the peak. In the 1960s, quicksand appeared in 3% of all films!

Much to my surprise, I never encountered quicksand as a child in the real world. Based on movies alone, I fully expected that my adult life would involve many encounters with the slippery stuff. Maybe that's why the image of cheerleading from quicksand came to me so vividly. Perhaps that's why I could feel the slippery sensation of my foundation shaking beneath me. As a child, I was prepared to move slowly and heroically pull myself out of the quicksand.

Recently, my daughter was watching *The Croods: Family Tree*[3] while I was trying to get work done. When the Crood family ran into quicksand, I perked up and paid attention. "It's not *quick*sand," Dad Crood said, "it's *slow* sand," as he steadily descended into the quagmire. And that's us, too. We miss the cues that we're sinking. Quicksand rarely announces its presence to us.

We want our minds to show a sign that says, "Caution, quicksand ahead!" But instead, we step into the quicksand and start to sink slowly, believing everything is fine until it's too late.

Despite my lack of experience in actual quicksand, I am pretty sure from my cinematic research that it isn't something you get out of quickly. Your exit from the slippery stuff can be messy, flailing, and stressful. The struggle to get out on your own only makes it harder to find your footing on solid ground, exhausting yourself in the process.

My hope is that my story helps you recognize the warning signs, find your way to solid ground, and understand what to do the next time you encounter quicksand. The goal is to help you make that exit a little more pleasant, much less messy, and with considerably less flailing.

We can't make our way out until we understand how we arrived in the quicksand. We'll begin by exploring how you ended up there in the first place: the burnout that pulls you into the muck. Together, we will work to understand it. We'll discuss the factors that create the perfect conditions for burnout. In the quicksand, I call these **Drain, Disconnect, and Doubt**. From there, we'll go through the three things that provide a way out of the bog. I call them the ABCs: **Authenticity, Boundaries, and Counterbalance**.

If you notice a pattern of threes, you're absolutely correct. As the youngest of three, I happen to believe that good things come in threes. You'll see this repeated throughout each section, with groups of three for each of the trials and tribulations of the quicksand (and that escape route I mentioned, too). My hope is that it means you have less to remember as you find your way forward.

As I was writing the book, I started to wonder if my quicksand experience was unique or if others had similar experiences. I surveyed friends, family, clients, and neighbors to hear about their experiences in the quicksand. You'll find their quotes woven throughout the book. Their names have been changed to protect their identity.

You'll also find sections called *Solid Ground* at the end of each chapter. These are intentional pauses, places to stop and reconnect with yourself. They include reflections, questions, and simple practices designed to help you notice what you need next. There's no right way to move through them. You don't need to complete every question or exercise all at once, or even in order. Take what feels useful, leave what doesn't, and return as often as you need.

As you move forward, I invite you to shift. Not just out of quicksand, but toward a life that feels like yours again. The *Solid Ground* section is your chance to zoom out, refocus, and realign, and design a steady foundation so you can move out of the quicksand and step into your best, most authentic life.

But first, we have to dive into the quicksand so that we can find our way out of it.

PART ONE

Into the Quicksand

CHAPTER 1

Burnout Outside of the Box

"It felt like everything was piling up on me at once, and it felt like everything was spiraling out of control with no light at the end of the tunnel."

That night in the bathroom felt dark, like I had fully sunk into quicksand with no hope of escape. When I realized something wasn't right, I immediately tried to identify the problem so I could start fixing it. That sentence tells you everything you need to know about me: even when I'm struggling, my first instinct is to get to work fixing things. Especially at that time, I was a people-pleasing, chronic perfectionist and fixer. Something was out of place, and I needed to correct it, but to do so, I needed to know the issue.

I knew I was grieving; that was clear. I also knew that I was in the thick of parenting young kids while building my career. Add in the chaos of a global pandemic, and I no longer recognized myself or my life. While trying to fix the problem, I leaned on what had always worked for me when I was stuck: research. Along the way, I stumbled upon the definition of burnout.

According to the World Health Organization (WHO), burnout is:

> *A syndrome conceptualized as resulting from chronic workplace stress that has not been successfully managed. It is characterized by three dimensions: 1) feelings of energy depletion or exhaustion, 2) increased mental distance from one's job, feelings of negativism or cynicism related to one's job and 3) a sense of ineffectiveness and lack of accomplishment. Burnout specifically refers to phenomena in an occupational context and should not be applied to describe experience in other areas of life. (ICD-11).*[4]

So much of this resonated with me: Exhausted emotions (check), cynicism (check), and feelings of ineffectiveness (check again). Up until that point in the definition, it felt like the WHO had been reading my emails. Finally, I had a word for what I was feeling. Then I reached the last sentence: "*Burnout specifically refers to phenomena in an occupational context and should not be applied to describe experience in other areas of life.*"

While I appreciate the use of the word *phenomena*, I had to call BS. My burnout has never been exclusive to my occupational context. According to my research, I'm not alone. Burnout permeates both sides of the work and life equation and rarely fits perfectly into one box or the other. So instead of trying to compartmentalize my burnout, I started to call it "Quicksand."

Quicksand is the thick, murky mess we find ourselves in when we've been burning the candle at both ends and in the middle. It symbolizes the all-consuming burnout from work, home, family, marriage, friends, health, mental health, and everything in between. It is the work stress that bleeds into your home life. It's the morning argument with a child about wearing a jacket that follows you to work. Thinking that these can be separated by category feels like fighting a losing battle when you're already battling enough. So we will tackle it all together as one thing and that thing is a sticky patch of quicksand.

Your very own personal patch of the muck is a mix that is unique to you and your pressures. The makeup changes over time and by season of life, but it is yours and yours alone. Congratulations! Like David Rose in *Schitt's Creek*, you just discovered land that is all your own. And yes, your quicksand can feel schitt-adjacent.

My quicksand looks like running a business and managing a household, keeping six creatures alive (seven if you count me, and I guess maybe I should), and driving all over town for my kids and my work. My husband's job requires him to travel full-time, so sometimes it involves time-bending and asking for a lot of help. Throw in a dash of insomnia, a sprinkle of caregiving for my parents, and a large serving of existential dread, and you get a pretty good understanding of what my quicksand is like. Your quicksand may have some overlap with mine, but it undoubtedly looks different. There will be parts of my story that don't resonate with you. Take what you need and leave the rest.

Let's revisit the World Health Organization's definition and its three dimensions of burnout: energy depletion, cynicism, and ineffectiveness. It's no joke that energy depletion is another way to say "exhaustion," because reading these components makes me tired. Even after all the research I have done, I stumble over the definition.

But what I remember most is how burnout makes me feel, like I am in quicksand: drained of energy, disconnected from others, and filled with doubt. So that's how we'll refer to them as we unpack the three dimensions of quicksand: **Drain, Disconnect, and Doubt.**

Drain describes the exhaustion that seeps into every corner of your life, like running on fumes no matter how much you rest. It's the physical, emotional, and mental depletion that makes even simple tasks feel heavy. Drain is where burnout begins, often silently, as you move through your days with less and less energy to spare. It might feel like the inertia that keeps you from getting up off the couch. Sometimes I just felt like I was *over it,* only *it* was most everything in my life. Drain can be a slight shift or a total loss of energy. You don't notice the quicksand at first; you just know that something isn't quite right.

Over time, that drain makes us want to protect our energy, and we do so by distancing ourselves from anyone and anything we perceive to be a threat to our energy. Disconnect happens when you begin to feel numb, cynical, or far away from the people and work that once mattered to you. Remember that the official definition calls it "depersonalization." It's the feeling that you're watching your life unfold from somewhere just outside of it. It is emotional distance disguised as efficiency. When you're disconnected, you stop feeling like yourself, and that loss of connection accelerates the sinking. Anyone who could possibly help us find a way out feels farther away than ever.

Once disconnect happens, doubt joins the party. Doubt, or what the WHO calls "ineffectiveness," shows up as the gradual erosion of your confidence, competence, and sense of worth. You begin to question your abilities, decisions, impact, and even your identity. Doubt convinces you that you can't pull yourself out of the quicksand, that you're too far in, and maybe you were never capable of escaping it anyway. It's the quiet voice that turns burnout from a season into a spiral.

Don't Take My Word for It

**If you heard this in LeVar Burton's voice, I probably need to apologize again for triggering your *NeverEnding Story* trauma, because you are likely an 80s kid too.

Ironically enough, writing a book about being in the quicksand brought back the old familiar feelings of doubt. Who am I to write a book? Why would anyone want to listen to me? I certainly knew that burnout wasn't unique to me, and that so many other people's lives were forever altered in the early 2020s. As I struggled with my feelings of doubt, I shared these feelings with a friend and she recommended that I lean into them. She suggested that I ask my friends, family, and followers about their experiences with quicksand.

I sent out a call for burnout stories and as usual, my village delivered. Former colleagues, past audience members, lifelong friends and fellow entrepreneurs chimed in to tell me about how they experienced burnout and how they found their way to the other side. It was heartbreaking to hear all the ways that people in my circle had navigated their own quicksand, often silently and alone.

A few common themes emerged that helped solidify that I was on the right track with how I defined what it felt like in the quicksand and the path to solid ground, so I wanted to hit the highlights here. I found it helpful to see it from the 50,000-foot view of their experiences.

Across the board, respondents described their journey into quicksand as a slow erosion of energy, confidence, and connection. Like me, so many didn't realize they were sinking until something broke: whether it was a relationship, a job, their health, or their sense of self. My feelings about the World Health Organization's definition of burnout as a work-related phenomenon were repeated as well: burnout affected career, caregiving, personal relationships, and everything in between. Maybe I tend to hang out with fellow overachievers, but so many also stayed in the muck for longer than necessary because they heard voices saying they *should* be able to handle everything that was thrown at them.

For many I surveyed, drain felt like utter tiredness, endless decision fatigue, a feeling of being "on" all the time and waking up worn out every day. An oil and gas executive said, "Days just kept running together. I constantly felt behind, reactive, not able to be in the moment or to put 100% into the current effort."

Disconnect for the respondents felt like a loss of empathy, going through the motions, or feeling like a shell of themselves. Like me, many experienced feelings of guilt about this withdrawal, especially those in caregiving roles. "I want to escape and not have anyone else dependent on me or my ideas" was the response of someone still navigating their path out of the quicksand.

Many reported feeling similar doubts too, believing they were replaceable, invisible, or that something was fundamentally wrong with them at their core. Others questioned their competence, despite evidence that clearly contradicted this feeling. One comment checked every box of drain, disconnect, and doubt: "I dreaded going into work. I felt nervous before every meeting and I didn't want to speak up or give my honest thoughts on things. I couldn't be myself."

Like my experience, survey respondents waited to seek help until the symptoms became unbearable. Internal pressure and identity attachment delayed their efforts even further. When they did start their recovery, many found that authenticity forged awareness, boundaries created space, and counterbalance supported sustainability.

Echoing my path forward, several recovery journeys started with the recognition that something wasn't right, centered around quiet, internal reflection. They shared stories of realizing they were living according to others' expectations. Naming this helped them identify what mattered most: family, health, meaning, and alignment. Interestingly, across the board this call-out came before action, creating clarity but not relief. The way forward began when people were truthful with themselves.

For many, that truth opened the door for joy. A fellow post-burnout solopreneur told me, "What was once a drain on my energy fuels me. I feel more creative than ever because no one is telling me no. There are no expectations, except the ones I allow. There are no politics to play. There are no unreasonable deadlines. I'm not working, I'm creating. Playing. And that's f*cking fun." Say it louder again for the ones stuck at the top of the corporate ladder, friend!

I know not everyone can say goodbye to the corporate overlords goodbye (although I would argue you can and should, but that's a story for another book). What we can do, and what many people have done on their way toward a new reality is create ground rules for living. The word "boundaries" came up in 55% of the survey responses, so even if that feels like a bad word to you, listen to what my fellow survivors told me.

A healthcare provider shared, "I had to set some boundaries related to where I put my energy." A fellow HR professional said what helped her was that she "finally set boundaries and stopped saying yes to everything." Other times, boundaries looked like reducing workloads or responsibilities, saying no without justifying or over-explaining, or letting go of expectations, internal or otherwise. It wasn't always comfortable, but the relief that resulted was always worth the discomfort.

Counterbalance was a clear theme in responses about their post-burnout lives; there was no return to "normal" but a renewed focus on investing in themselves. Seeking joy without permission, inviting rest and support, and rebuilding routines to replenish energy showed up in response to the question about where they were in their burnout journey.

I wanted to cheer when I read a former client's response that perfectly summarized what happens when we invite help: "It always feels like there is some sort of fire going on but now I have a strong team in place. We can lean on each other for support. Before it was a raging bonfire, now it's just a few smaller fires that we can tackle together." Seeking support definitely helps, but a fellow author/entrepreneur reminded me, "while you may receive support and assistance, you are the only one who can take control of your life and resolve the burnout."

That responsibility came through in responses focused on avoiding quicksand and not sliding back into old habits. Even those who feel stable continue to monitor. A recovering workaholic said, "I'm also not going to let myself get to that place again." A family member said, "it's easy to fall into old patterns and disregard my own boundaries." Those who are still navigating the quicksand are mindful of the choices that they make as they continue finding a way forward. One respondent summed it up perfectly: "Still healing but better! It takes practice and time. Doing better with boundaries and choosing where my energy goes when I have the option."

Realizing that I wasn't alone made me feel so much better about my experience, and that is my goal for you in reading this book, to feel less alone. In the pages ahead, we'll dive into the three Ds that pull you under. Then we will break down the ABCs that lift you out so you can find your footing again and move toward a life that feels not only steadier, but also more authentic to you.

SOLID GROUND

What's in Your Quicksand?

Instructions: Review the categories below. For each, rate how much it's currently pulling you under using the scale:

0 - Not a problem
1 - Mild drag
2 - Noticeable weight
3 - Heavy burden
4 - Totally weighed down

Category	Description	Rating 0-4
The Workload	Job demands, team tension, leadership stress, entrepreneurship pressure	
The People Load	Family, caregiving, emotional labor, friends, social strain	
The Homefront	Chores, errands, clutter, home maintenance, life admin	
The Money Mess	Bills, financial uncertainty, budgeting, debt	
The Body & Brain	Physical health, sleep, mental health, burnout symptoms	
The Bigger Picture	News, global stress, politics, societal instability	

Reflection

1. Which three categories weigh you down the most?
2. Where do you have the most control?
3. Where could a change make the biggest impact?
4. Where do you feel you have the least influence at this moment?
5. What weights are you able to set down, even temporarily?
6. What items are seasonal or temporary?
7. What kinds of supports would be helpful to identify in each category?
8. If you had a magic wand and could fix one of these issues, which one would you choose?

....

CHAPTER 2

Low Battery, High Expectations

"I didn't want to get out of bed in the morning. I dreaded every single day. I was also forced to keep going for others. Thankfully, that also kept me going for myself. But it was exhausting, and my health suffered greatly."

Drain

Imagine a quicksand scene in a movie, any movie. As we discussed, you have plenty of options. Think about how the character moved once they realized where they were. You'll probably remember some flailing: people stuck in a mess, but don't know how to escape. They usually pick the option that involves wildly thrashing about in hopes of miraculously escaping. Instead, they exhaust themselves and probably sink even lower. Now, not only are they still stuck, but they are also drained of energy to do anything productive next.

Sound familiar? That's what happens when we find ourselves stuck in the emotional quicksand of burnout. We try everything to escape, only to find ourselves deeper and drained of the ability to take the next step. It looks like mental and physical exhaustion that seeps into our work, life, and everything in between. The slow, silent nature of it means we are in a deep puddle before we even realize we are in it.

Drain also occurs in situations where we are required to be emotionally "on" for long periods. Anyone leading a team, organization, or household knows exactly what I mean. "Smiles, everybody, smiles. I've got this, and there's no need to worry." You keep telling yourself that until eventually you don't believe it anymore. Like a light that stays on too long, it begins to dim and it will eventually burn out.

For me, drain felt like my energy was being sucked out, along with my will to do more than just the bare minimum. I imagined a washcloth that started out soaking wet, but by the end of the day, it was bone-dry and crunchy. When I got home, I was completely drained like the washcloth, nothing left to give to anyone, including myself. I began with the goal of being there for everyone, and I like to think I did my best at the time. But there was never enough energy left at day's end.

A few months ago, my car started hesitating just a little when I tried to start it. I could mostly ignore it, but when it happened in a parking lot 100 miles from home, I knew I needed to resolve the issue. My husband started troubleshooting it by turning it off and on about a dozen times, and it never happened to him. He said it was probably just a glitch, and it was fine. He told me to just "hold down the start button a little longer," and he is lucky I love him enough to let him mansplain my car to me.

The next time it happened, I drove straight to an auto shop. Diagnostics showed my battery was at 50% capacity, and I needed a new one. When I called my husband to cash in my "I told you so" check, he said, "It started every time I tried, so I just thought it was okay." That statement perfectly summed up what happens when we are feeling drained: running at half capacity but going through our days anyway until we finally can't pretend any longer.

Just like the car battery, operating at a minimal capacity wears us down. Drain acts as a warning sign of other components. Understanding and recognizing the drain can help you realize that you are sinking into quicksand. Unfortunately, drain also prevents us from realizing what we are experiencing, just like my battery at half-capacity.

When we are drained, the brain's amygdala (which processes emotions like fear and anxiety) becomes overactive, while the prefrontal cortex (which manages rational thinking and self-control) becomes less effective. This neurological shift caused by emotional exhaustion makes it harder to regulate emotions, leading to irritability, overwhelm, and eventual shutdown. Physically, it might trigger headaches, digestive issues, or insomnia. Drain feels like the kind of tiredness that sleep doesn't help, even though you might be sleeping more than usual to fix or escape it.

It is most common among females experiencing burnout, and that rang true in my research. Almost every woman who responded to my survey told stories of feeling drained. One respondent recounted a moment from the quicksand and said,

> "I was hyper-stressed. Any little thing would set me off. I felt like I was standing in the middle of the room screaming, but no one could hear me. I felt like I was on the verge of a complete mental and emotional breakdown. The phone calls and texts were coming through non-stop. It seemed that everyone needed a piece of me, pieces that I no longer had to give."

Anecdotally, I notice that the women in my life (including myself) tend to shoulder more of the emotional labor and mental load at home. We are the keepers of household knowledge, calendars, and emotions. I often say that I am both the head and the heart, remembering to make the dentist appointments and to ensure the tooth fairy has cash. It is up to me to remember the date and time for the birthday party, purchase a gift, and comfort my child when they return with stories of the bully at the party. Even with a very engaged and helpful spouse, I once calculated that I spend roughly 24 hours per week in the business of mental load, and honestly, that number seems low.

Existing research confirmed this sentiment. The Family Caregiver Alliance estimates that 66% of caregivers are female and that female caregivers spend up to 50% more time providing care than male caregivers.[5] Additionally, a recent literature review found that women perform a higher proportion of mental labor, especially for childcare and parenting decisions. This imbalance leads to more stress, lower satisfaction in work and life, and negative effects on their careers.[6]

Over time, carrying that load and being "on" all the time can take a toll. Art imitates life through numerous books and movies about women who reach their limit and escape their own lives. The 2025 Christmas movie *Oh. What. Fun.* offers a perfect example of a mom who reaches her tipping point and (spoiler alert) runs away from her unappreciative family.

This isn't to say that men can't also experience emotional drain and that women don't also exhibit other factors. We do win this round in terms of prevalence, except it's not really a win. Regardless of gender, emotional drain worsens our health. One study found that, due to prolonged burnout, it leads to headaches, fatigue, sleep disruptions, and muscle tension.[7] That same study found that every one-point increase in burnout was associated with a one-unit increase in the risk of hospitalization for cardiovascular problems. Again and again, the research tells us that drain negatively impacts our physical health.

The acquisition of the company drained me on all fronts. I spent my days acting completely at odds with my natural management style. When I was at my best, I was a transparent, inclusive, and empowering leader. The challenges of the merger meant I had to be secretive, restrictive, and closed off from my team. Where I was normally involved and engaged, walking around and checking in on everyone, I instead retreated to my office and tried to conserve my energy. I busied myself with calls and projects that didn't require me to put on a face or be present with my people.

This was counterintuitive for me because I get my energy from other people. Literally every assessment I have ever taken shows me falling at the far end of the extroversion spectrum, meaning I find energy and enjoyment in the external world and with other people. Emotional drain took that from me. Every time I retreated, I would further deplete what I had left, all because I thought I was protecting myself.

The more I tried to conserve my energy, the more drained I felt. In my journey out of the quicksand, I realized inauthenticity was kerosene on the burnout. It was the force that pulled me deeper into the quicksand. I was mentally, physically, and emotionally drained from not being my true, authentic self.

As the acquisition progressed, I realized the new company's personality didn't align with my authentic self either. In its previous iteration, we operated as an involved and engaged leadership team. The new normal meant more calls with corporate, more time spent in closed-door offices, and less focus on employee engagement. Meetings and projects with my team were replaced with reports and metrics. Things I thought were temporary symptoms of the merger became permanent expectations. The longer I had to pretend to be someone I wasn't, the more drained I became. I was short-fused with my family because the more time I spent in that mode, the less energy I had to do even the things I loved.

These feelings came up in so much of my research. My friend Lynn responded to my survey about burnout and told me:

> "Burnout for me is being emotionally fatigued. When I begin to "crash" and fall asleep before 7:00 pm, I sleep for 4 to 5 hours. I also experience increased irritability. I notice that everyone/everything annoys me, including the people who never do. I have reached a point of significant distress. A typical day is being on autopilot… My day can feel kind of directionless, as though I am just standing there, not sure what to do next."

That perfectly sums up the quicksand for me, too: physically and emotionally worn out and unsure what to do next. It looked like standing in my bathroom and feeling like I was in a hole. I had no idea how I was going to get out, but I knew that I couldn't continue with the way things were.

The recognition in that moment didn't give me the answers I needed to find my way out, but I did start asking different questions about what got me there. That seemingly small shift created the foothold that would eventually lead me out of the quicksand and onto solid ground.

SOLID GROUND

Drain

1. What does drain look like for you:
   - Physically?
   - Mentally?
   - Emotionally?

2. Where do you feel it first? Where does it linger the longest?

3. Where is your battery today?
   - 100% • 50% • Barely charging • Running on fumes and coffee

4. What is your default response to drain? Do you:
   - Power through?
   - Withdraw?
   - Ignore the warning altogether?

5. In what ways does prolonged drain pull you away from your true, authentic self?

6. What parts of you go quiet when you're exhausted?

7. What mental load responsibilities or thoughts are currently "running in the background" for you?

Disconnect

"Over time, a feeling of being consistently overlooked and unappreciated eroded my motivation, and I began to disengage. It resulted in a period where I was simply going through the motions."

The quicksand is a lonely place. Dark, uncomfortable, and seemingly endless, it isn't exactly where we feel like having company. When we slip into quicksand, we pull away from the people in our lives, detach, and retreat into solitude. When emotional exhaustion reaches a tipping point, the brain's limbic system (responsible for emotional regulation) shuts down non-essential emotional responses as a protective measure. This is a psychological defense mechanism that causes us to withdraw from friends, colleagues, and loved ones. As a result, we see people as problems rather than human beings, which leads to detachment, cynicism, and resentment. In short, *if I don't care so much, you can't hurt me so badly.*

My son taught me that when sharks fight, they form a protective film over their eyes to prevent getting them poked out. Disconnect, the second phase of burnout, is your body's equivalent of that film. Your brain protects you from feeling overwhelmed by numbing your emotions. What seems like an effective way to stay safe can actually leave you feeling alone and isolated over time. That protective film is meant to be temporary, but keeping your guard up for too long brings you down.

Disconnect might sound like sarcasm and cynicism. It might look like avoidance or procrastination. It is related to compassion fatigue, a condition that leads to a diminished ability to empathize or care. This fatigue is common in caregiving professions where people are constantly supporting others through challenging times. Eventually, detachment erodes job satisfaction and personal well-being, and it can lead to diminished patient outcomes.

One survey respondent shared her story from the quicksand that illustrated the path from drain to disconnect.

"At its worst, I could not emotionally get through simple interactions. I could pretend in the moment, but would leave the experience and cry, or on a few occasions, experience panic attacks… It meant a loss of love for a career that had once overflowed me with joy. I could do the work in my sleep, but I found no fulfillment in my day-to-day any longer. It felt like a loss. My burnout was particularly career-focused but it caused me to gain weight and be a poor version of myself in relationships."

That resonated so much with my experience. It looked like a lack of connection. I separated myself from my colleagues, friends, and family as a defense mechanism. I was totally drained of the energy to give any more, and I felt like if I separated myself from everyone, it wouldn't be so obvious that I was on autopilot. The peak of my burnout coincided with COVID, so it was really easy to separate myself from everyone. Retreating to my office, hunkering down at home all weekend, and declining socially distanced invitations became my reality. Like taking an old-school phone off its receiver, I sent out a signal that I couldn't be reached, and I separated myself from everyone else.

Over time, this disconnect created an isolation that made it harder to get out of the quicksand. Where I normally would've had friends noticing that I wasn't myself, I didn't give them opportunities to witness it. Had I maintained connection with others, they likely would have recognized that I needed support as I navigated my grief. Without that separation that disconnect created, I began to doubt that I would ever find my way back into the light.

SOLID GROUND

Disconnect

1. When you're feeling disconnected, how do you protect yourself or your energy? What do you pull away from, avoid, or keep at arm's length?

2. How does disconnection show up in your voice or behavior? Do you sound more:
   - Cynical?
   - Defeated?
   - Guarded?
   - Numb?
   - Overly efficient?
   - Unusually quiet?

3. Who do you feel most disconnected from right now (others, your work, or yourself)? What do you miss about that connection?

4. In what ways is this disconnection keeping you trapped in quicksand? What feels more difficult, heavy, or lonely because of it?

5. Who in your circle feels safe or supportive enough to reconnect with this season? What would support from them actually entail (listening, encouragement, shared laughter, practical help)?

Doubt

"New projects weren't fun challenges anymore, but rather dreaded tasks. I was constantly in a negative headspace and stressed out. I would tie my self-worth to my work and spiral, because I felt like I was failing and drowning."

We've talked about how quicksand leaves us tired and separated from others, but there's one more component that contributes to it. It's the feeling that, despite trying your hardest to push through the challenges, none of it seems to have an impact. After a while, you begin to feel that your work is ineffective, meaningless, or that no one cares.

This causes the brain's dopamine system (which regulates motivation and reward) to become dysregulated, making it harder to feel a sense of progress or satisfaction. This creates self-doubt, a decrease in confidence that perpetuates the belief that nothing you do makes a difference. Simply buying into the doubt can make it come true, a self-fulfilling prophecy, especially when coupled with drain and disconnect. This can lead to learned helplessness, a psychological state where repeated stress and setbacks make a person believe their efforts are futile.

Two survey respondents shared stories about how doubt affected their ability to function. One responded, "*I just shut down with no effort to follow through on my commitments.*" The other described doubt as causing "*paralysis some days, procrastination at the lightest end, and a full emotional nervous breakdown at the hardest end.*"

You have probably felt this self-doubt before. The quicksand version looks like comparing yourself negatively to others, which decreases confidence in your abilities and skills. This component leads to a loss of motivation, leaving you with no interest in doing much of anything. You might find yourself avoiding tasks, even ones you know you are capable of, because they seem pointless.

In the quicksand, I doubted my choices at work regarding pandemic protocols. I questioned my ability to lead the organization through so much change. I self-selected out of opportunities, feeling like I could never meet expectations, something I had never faced in my career. Doubt became my default emotion, making every decision much more difficult because I had to slog through my own hangups at every turn.

Looking back, I also realize I had taken on more than I could possibly manage. I was trying to carry a full load and do it flawlessly. Instead of questioning whether I was taking on too much, I looked for work/life balance strategies. This was not a new quest for me; even my graduate thesis focused on work-life balance, and I continued to learn as much as I could about the promised land of equilibrium between work and life for over a decade. Despite my extensive research, I never found a system, planner, process, or life hack to balance it all.

When I couldn't accomplish that mythical balance, I convinced myself something was wrong with me, leading me right back to doubt. So, if you're keeping track, I was exhausted, alone, and didn't believe I was capable of ever escaping. In short, I was drained, disconnected, and full of doubt.

SOLID GROUND

Doubt

1. What does doubt sound like in your head right now? What questions, criticisms, or "not enough" stories keep repeating?

2. Where have you started to question your competence, confidence, or worth?

3. What once felt natural or energizing that now feels heavy or uncertain?

4. In what areas of your life are you trying to be too much for too many people? Where has stretching yourself thin begun to look like commitment, responsibility, or leadership?

5. How is doubt keeping you stuck in quicksand? What risks are you no longer taking, or what decisions are you delaying because you don't trust yourself?

6. If doubt loosened its grip even slightly, what might become possible again? What would you do differently if you believed you were already enough?

A Pause Before We Find Our Way Out

Friends, we made it through the trifecta of quicksand's troubles. You may have come to the realization that you are, in fact, stuck in the quicksand. You're drained. You're struggling to connect with your friends, family, and colleagues, and you're doubting yourself and the impact you're making. If you're anything like me, you're also cheering on everyone else in your life, trying to hold people up while sinking as well.

If learning about the quicksand feels heavy, that's because it is. Pause here and go get a little treat. While you're up, grab one for me! If you've come here because you are so deep in the quicksand that you can't find the light, I see you. Maybe you only feel up to reading the Solid Ground sections to start. Or, this might be as far as you are ready to go right now, and kudos to you for realizing that and making it to this point. This is your journey and yours alone, so take it at whatever pace feels right for you. I will be ready to cheer you on whenever you are ready to restart.

But if you think you can keep going, let's talk about finding our way out of it. It's time to solidify your foundation so you can continue cheering for the people in your life.

PART TWO

Out of the Quicksand

CHAPTER 3

And Now, Back to You

As I navigated my way out of the ***drain, disconnect, and doubt*** that is quicksand, I found myself repeating a few strategies that finally gave me relief. They included showing up as my full self, protecting my peace, and taking a more holistic approach to balancing my responsibilities. Over time, I identified that these strategies fell neatly into a set of ABCs: **Authenticity, Boundaries, and Counterbalance.** Each of the three ABCs pairs with its own component of the quicksand. ***Authenticity*** beats ***drain***, ***boundaries*** help solve the ***disconnect***, and ***counterbalance*** is the answer to ***doubt***.

Where ***drain*** causes energy depletion, ***authenticity*** rebuilds your reserves. When you reconnect with your core values, show up as your real self, and stop performing for the approval of others, your mental and emotional energy begins to return. ***Authenticity*** restores the parts of you that the drain takes from you, helping you stand tall again. It comes first because it creates resilience for everything to come after you find solid ground.

Disconnect tells you that the only safe way to conserve your energy is to separate from everyone around you. ***Boundaries*** create a blueprint for engaging with others without sacrificing yourself. They protect your time, your emotional bandwidth, and your relationships from overextension that leads to resentment and distance. They can be rules of engagement with others or for how you treat yourself and protect your total health. Boundaries reconnect you to yourself and to others in a healthier, more sustainable way.

Where ***doubt*** makes you believe you don't have what it takes to navigate your way out, ***counterbalance*** creates stability to carry you through. When you ease the load that you carry, evaluate what matters, and make space to enjoy your life again, you rebuild trust in your ability to navigate hard seasons. ***Counterbalance*** gives you tools to steady yourself so you don't topple under the weight of everything you carry.

You learned your ABCs a long time ago, but let's relearn them together as a way to get back to solid ground.

Authenticity

"It doesn't necessarily mean you crash out and can't get out of bed. Sometimes it feels like the light is just a little dimmer than it used to be…in almost every area of life."

Authenticity is the first foothold out of the quicksand. It is the moment you stop performing for the world and start listening to yourself again. Trying to be someone you aren't is exhausting; it is no wonder you feel drained. That's why we begin here, with the work of returning to who you are, so you have the energy you need.

When I realized I was in the quicksand, I only knew two things for certain about my job: I couldn't keep doing it, and if I was going to leave my corporate job, I needed to start my own business. Makes perfect sense, right? I was at maximum capacity, so why not embark on something big and daunting like starting a company? My reason for doing it was so much bigger than the reasons not to, and that was my brother.

For as long as I can remember, I have dreamed of owning my own business. When I was in college, I would drive by this nondescript building with a person's name on the door, and I would think *how cool they get to do that*. Yes, I now know that it isn't that glamorous, and that it was a nerdy thing for a college kid to be impressed by, but that's how much I wanted to be my own boss.

When I was interviewed for that first HR role at the infusion pharmacy, the company owners asked where I saw myself in five years. I answered honestly and said, "I want to own my own business." Was this a terrible answer to an interview question? Yes. But it was also authentic. To their credit, they said, "Great! Run ours first and see what you think. When we sell it, you can run your own!"

Spoiler alert: I eventually did exactly that. I never would have imagined that along the way, I would ascend to the COO level. The time I spent working with the first owners of the infusion pharmacy was some of the most impactful years of my career, and I always look back on that interview with so much gratitude. Working with the new company versus working with them was jarring to say the least.

One of my last conversations with my late brother, Jay, was about this longtime dream of owning my own business. We were out to dinner during the trip that ended up being our final family vacation. Jay and I ended up in a sidebar conversation, and being the baby of the family, I knew that one-on-one time with my big brother was solid gold. Every conversation with him was peppered with gentle guidance and support.

I was about six months into my role at the newly merged company. I told him I was hopeful things would get better, but it didn't seem promising. We started talking about whether it was time for me to take the leap, and when I say "leap," I mean a giant step out of the comfort zone of a corporate leadership role (and the salary, bonus, and benefits that came with it). He was realistic, but also wholeheartedly believed I could do it. His belief made me feel like nothing was impossible.

When I lost Jay and his encouragement, I lost the will to start something new. I now know I was so deep in the quicksand that I forgot about that version of myself, the authentic one who wanted to be a business owner. I put it on the back burner and chose the stability of a corporate role for a while. The monotony of a 9-to-5, the comfort of my team, and the structure that the job provided were a good fit for that period of my life where I was engulfed in grief. But as time went on, that conversation kept coming back: *take the leap.*

I told my corporate boss in mid-2022 that I was ready to leave, but I wanted to do so in a way that would cause the least disruption. The organization and my team had already been through a lot, and I wanted to be there, pom-poms in hand, as long as I could. Together, my boss and I created a three-month transition plan for me to go from full-time to part-time in July, then fully leave in October. It was the perfect slow roll into starting my own business. They also made it incredibly easy to detach emotionally when they sent the letter that confirmed my termination. It was addressed to "Zavy Lurch." Yes, first name Zavy, last name Lurch. If nothing else, it was a clear sign: corporate overlords will never love you back, so you might as well do what brings you joy.

Once the company gave me (or, Zavy Lurch) that final push, I needed to create a business, including giving it a name. Unfortunately, I was stuck. I couldn't find anything that fit what I wanted to convey, and I kept wishing I could just ask my brother for his advice. I lamented to my husband Brad one night that I was never supposed to do this without Jay and that maybe it was a sign I shouldn't do it at all. Brad reminded me to be patient, to listen, and trust that it would come.

One of the things that supported me through grief was nightly meditation, a practice my brother had also taken on when he got sick. During a meditation one night, almost like a whisper, I heard *"rivers and roads."* It was a line from a song my siblings and I loved, and it connected to one of the last things I said to Jay. At that moment, I knew I had my company name.

When I tell you things come together when you start living authentically, I really mean it. So in summary, quit your job, meditate, and start a company named after your favorite song. Thank you for coming to my TED Talk.

I kid, I kid. What I am serious about is that we have to examine where we are and who we aspire to be to move out of the quicksand. Drain tells us we don't have the energy to be anything other than an exhausted shell of ourselves. Authenticity reminds us that there is a much better, truer version of ourselves waiting on the other side. When you remember that person, you begin noticing what is meant for you. For me, it meant pursuing the dream of starting my own company. For you, it might be reconnecting with your love of swimming. Or asking for that raise you deserve. Once you begin to hear your inner voice, it will remind you of those dreams and your potential. And if you listen, you will slowly begin coming back to yourself.

A few months after quitting my job, my mom was at my house during the after-school chaos. It was a time when I would normally still have been at the office, working until the last possible moment before I had to pick up my kids. Instead, I was fixing snacks, moving laundry between rooms, and cracking jokes with my kids.

My mom looked at me, shook her head, and said, "Do you have any idea how different you are?" I was relaxed, present, and actually enjoying the moment. I hadn't yet noticed the shift in myself, but she did. Looking back, it was the first time in a long time I remember feeling lighter.

If I had followed the "shoulds," I would have taken another job just like the one I left and found my way right back in the quicksand. But instead, I silenced the noise of expectations and norms long enough to hear a whisper that told me I was on the right path.

Authenticity in Action

The noise makes it hard to believe that authenticity is even possible, and it all feels vague until you put it into motion. During my recovery from quicksand, authenticity revealed some recurring themes: **Purpose, Presence, and Permission.** These patterns emerged as I began to rebuild my foundation and kept me moving forward. It meant that I revisited my identity and became more grounded in that version of myself. I started to live my life out loud and trusted my own voice again. This practice, repeated over time, yielded a more authentic version of myself. I began to return to the person I was before the overwhelm of COVID and my grief.

When you begin leaning into all three, you create space for what matters most, and the drain begins to slow. When you release the pressure to follow someone else's definition of success, you begin building a path that feels like your own. Authenticity isn't about breaking every rule or reinventing your personality; it's about quietly reclaiming the freedom to choose how you want to live.

Purpose

Burnout pulls us away from who we are. When you're stuck in quicksand, you're farthest from your values, living a life of survival, not purpose. Reclaiming authenticity starts with a simple but profound question: What actually matters to me?

Answering that question brought me back to my brother, to the dreams we talked about the last time we were together, and to the truth that life is incredibly short. I realized I was spending my life in ways that didn't reflect what I value: being present with my family, doing meaningful work, and having the freedom to choose what my days look like. Something needed to change to allow me the space to live in alignment with my values.

You don't need a life-altering moment to gain clarity; you just need honesty about who you are, what values you hold, and why you are here. Simple, right?! It requires some time, reflection, and introspection. It involves remembering when you were happiest, asking yourself what conditions allow you to be at your best, and reconnecting with friends and family who remind you of your true self.

Once you have at least a sense of the answers, authenticity means aligning your days with those values, even in small ways. Many of us chase what we think we're "supposed" to want: titles, paychecks, prestige. But purpose, lived authentically, is simply remembering your "why" and letting it guide your choices again. From there, you reintroduce that version of yourself to the world.

Presence

Presence is how you show up, both internally and externally. I once thought this was the shallow category of authenticity, but showing up as someone you are not is possibly the most exhausting way to move through the world. Are you shrinking yourself so others stay comfortable? Are you performing a polished version of yourself that no longer fits? Looking back, I now see that I was doing both.

For years, I muted my authentic self to blend into rooms I wanted to impress. I straightened my wild curls every day because "professional" felt synonymous with "polished into submission." During this journey into authenticity, I embraced my natural curls for the first time in four decades. Letting them show was a small change, but it unlocked a freedom I didn't know I needed. It reminded me daily that I didn't have to perform anymore.

When I speak on stages and in workshops about authenticity, I ask participants to imagine their *authentic avatar*. I encourage them to think about what they would wear, how they would introduce themself, and how they would spend their time.

The answers are always beautiful and often surprisingly simple. Wearing their favorite accessory every day. A bolder voice. A schedule that respects their energy. Time spent in nature. It's rarely a reinvention, rather a gentle return. Sometimes I offer the option to draw their authentic avatar. When I drew mine, I noticed that the stick person version that I draw of myself has always had wild curly hair. It was this realization that gave me the permission to return to my (curly) roots.

Permission

Sometimes at the dinner table, my daughter will raise her hand to speak, forgetting that she is no longer in the classroom. That habit holds on tight, and into adulthood, we can still find ourselves waiting for permission. To speak up, to dissent, to go against the crowd. The first step out of the quicksand is to stop waiting for permission from others. We don't need someone else's approval to move forward, to say no, to design a life that reflects our rhythms, or permission to create boundaries that serve us. Somewhere along the way, we forgot that we own our own destiny. We aren't at the mercy of others' expectations or wants.

To me, permission looked like creating a schedule that supported the life I actually wanted. It meant honoring the way I work best, choosing joy when I could, and letting go of expectations I never agreed to in the first place. It involved rewriting the narrative and making sure I was the main character in my story. I make sure I am the one in charge of my schedule and routines, not someone else's, and certainly not someone's idea of what life should look like.

I ask my daughter all the time, "Who gave you permission to be so cute?" She always answers, "I did!" like it's the most obvious thing in the world. And she's right. The permission comes from within, we just need to remember to act on it.

Remember Lynn, who shared her feelings of drain earlier? When I asked her what helped her start recovering, she said: "When I began feeling increased frustration and resentment, I knew it was time for a change. Also, I know this is a common phrase, but 'life's too short' became a common thought related to family, which influenced my perspective. Feeling like myself again is a process that requires me to strengthen my connection with myself too."

One of the most pivotal books I read while climbing out of the quicksand was *Burnout,* written by sisters Emily and Amelia Nagoski. Lynn's comments reminded me so much of my favorite quote from the book: *"You are not here to be 'productive.' You are here to be you, to engage with your Something Larger, to move through the world with confidence and joy."*[8]

When we reflect on what brings us joy and where we find confidence, we start to climb out of the quicksand. For me, that climb actually meant getting off the ladder altogether and charting my own path. I believe you can do both—stay on the ladder and find your way out of the quicksand—but it requires intentionality and a commitment to seeking a solid footing.

What would it look like to give yourself permission? Where have you been waiting for someone to tell you it is okay to be someone, do something, or act on a dream? You can put your hand down now. You are the person you have been waiting for all along.

Stepping Onto Solid Ground

The journey toward authenticity doesn't come with a clear roadmap. It is a path you chart for yourself. And even once you find what you are looking for, you will still find more quicksand. That's why authenticity is the first step. It's the moment you stop sinking and start finding your footing again. When your decisions align with your values, when you show up as yourself instead of performing, when you grant yourself permission to live by your own rhythms, you create the first patch of solid ground beneath you.

The good news? Once authenticity takes root, you're no longer fighting blindly. You know who you are and what matters. From there, you can see where the disconnect is happening and challenge the doubt that's been whispering in your ear far too long. Authenticity doesn't solve everything. But it gives you something burnout steals: a place to begin.

But emerging from quicksand doesn't happen all at once. Authenticity helps you stand, but the next part of the journey asks you to look around and notice the forces that keep you stuck: disconnect and doubt.

SOLID GROUND

Authenticity

1. When do you feel most like yourself? What moments, environments, or roles bring out your energy, clarity, or ease?

2. At your core, who are you and what truly matters to you? Which values feel essential right now, even if your life doesn't fully reflect them yet?

3. What messages have you internalized about what you *should* value, prioritize, or pursue? Which of those beliefs feel misaligned with who you actually are?

4. How do you show up when you are at your best, your most grounded, most real?

5. If you imagine your authentic avatar:
   - What would they wear?
   - How would they introduce themselves?
   - Where would they spend their time and energy?

6. What permission have you been waiting for? Whose voices or expectations are guiding your decisions right now, and which ones no longer have a vote?

7. Where does your life currently feel misaligned with who you are becoming? What is one small way you could choose yourself more honestly?

CHAPTER 4

Ding-dong, Boundaries Calling

"Poor boundaries and wanting to say 'yes' to everything led to my burnout. It caused anxiety, feelings of overwhelm, and avoidance."

Boundaries get a bad rap, and I can understand why. They feel cold, rigid, and a little like like confrontation wearing a business suit. But what I know to be true about this quicksand is that the deeper we sink, the more we begin to disconnect. Pulling away might feel like relief, but all it really does is separate us from our village, from our cheerleaders, from the people who anchor us. What I've learned on my way out of the quicksand is that boundaries are essential to our survival.

Yes. Those boundaries. The lines you draw in the sand with your boss or with your coworkers. Holding firm on your response to your children's pleading. It's the agreements that you make with your sister (there are always boundaries with your sister). They are the boundaries that probably make you uncomfortable. But stay with me. I think we can navigate a way out of that discomfort. If you still hate them by the end of this chapter, I will happily accept your hate mail.

A few years ago, while preparing for a speaking engagement for a big client, I ran a practice session for friends and family. My mom came along, proud as ever, and after listening and nodding along, she had one comment. She said in total disbelief, "Boundaries?! We didn't have boundaries when I was raising kids!"

She said it the same way I tell my kids we didn't have iPhones when I was their age: matter-of-fact and absolute. And she's not wrong. My family did not have boundaries, and my therapy bill agrees.

My mom's observation was that there were no boundaries in the '80s, but honestly, I'm not sure the 2020s have boundaries either. Our lives revolve around our kids' schedules, the 27 unread emails (or **shudder** 9,999), the never-ending group texts, people we haven't seen since we wore butterfly clips sliding into our DMs with a sales pitch, and an endless loop of expectations we never signed up for. We are trying to operate in a world that demands more than any one person can reasonably give. We can't manufacture time, but learning how to set and uphold clear boundaries comes shockingly close.

Okay, what is a boundary?

My first foray into boundaries came from T*he Book of Boundaries*, by Melissa Urban. You may know Melissa from Whole 30 fame, that diet where you cut out wheat, sugar, dairy, alcohol, delight, etc. for 30 days. I've attempted the Whole 30 a few times with varying success and while I love the idea of it, I have never made it all the way through. The best thing about it was it led me to Melissa's socials and writing. Her book came at precisely the right time, as I was embarking on my entrepreneurial journey and working my way out of the quicksand.

The dictionary defines a boundary as "something that indicates or fixes a limit or extent." This definition works great in the context of physical boundaries like state lines and property limits, but things get more complicated when we start talking about two people interacting. The (Melissa) Urban Dictionary expands this to explain that interpersonal boundaries define where our identity, responsibility, and control begin and end relative to someone else.[9]

A boundary conveys what the other person can expect when interacting with you. It clarifies what you can do, how you expect to be treated, and what belongs in your lane. What it doesn't do is say "here's how you must behave in order to interact with me." Boundaries never override someone else's free will; they only clarify your own and give you a roadmap for how to voice your needs.

While I navigated my way out of the quicksand, I realized that I had become disconnected from the people who asked more of me than I was comfortable with or able to give. Whether it was a commitment I made Before Grief (BG), or overperforming to maintain a relationship, these demands began to wear on me. My energy was siphoned into places I didn't consciously agree to (or maybe I did, but I was ready to revoke that permission), and I felt the need to protect myself from the energy drain caused by such demands. These expectations made me cynical and distant. I felt like I needed to disconnect or withdraw, when what I needed was a boundary.

People often tell me they avoid boundaries because they "want to be nice," and I assure you that I have been there too. The belief that I had to be nice and make everyone happy ended up making me want to disconnect from others. Even when I knew I was sinking, I continued to overperform and exhaust myself further. Instead of speaking up, I retreated and disconnected from my team. It was as though I chose not to be present because I couldn't be perfect, but the result only made me feel more alone. I didn't want to rock the boat when large requests were made of my team or me, so I continued in quiet resentment.

The truth is that boundaries are not the opposite of kindness; boundaries *are* kindness. They help relationships flourish rather than fracture. They create clarity and awareness, setting limits around expectations, including your own. In my work and life, I've found that boundaries tend to fall into three categories: **Relationships, Resilience, and Renewal.** Each one asks something slightly different of you, but together they form the foundation that keeps you from sinking back into the quicksand.

Relationship Boundaries

Boundaries with other people often get a bad reputation because of how they are perceived in the first place. When most of us think about interpersonal boundaries, our minds jump to the kind that feel uncomfortable, confrontational, or even mean. To be fair, these are some of the hardest boundaries to set, but they don't have to be harsh. They are clear, kind, and establish ground rules for how you will interact. They aren't apologies, excuses, or long, drawn-out explanations. They reestablish the ground rules for how you interact with others and clarify roles, expectations, and understanding within a relationship.

They also help you eliminate things that no longer belong to you (or never should have in the first place). I find that disconnection often comes from overwhelm. When you're doing too much and trying to complete too many things, it's time to set a boundary. When you're roped into things you wouldn't volunteer for, it's time to set a boundary. When you want to screen that person's calls every single time, you guessed it, it's time for a boundary.

As you work to exit the quicksand, you'll also add new things along the way. These are conencted to the reinvention of your authentic self, and things like movement and self-care, that we will talk about in later chapters. You're also already carrying a full load to begin with: your own grief, stressors, and frustrations don't just disappear because you are doing the work to get out of the muck. You'll need room on your plate to carry those, and boundaries will give you that because you're removing the weight of other people's expectations. You're subtracting the time people have taken from you, whether consciously or subconsciously, that you need to put back into your life.

Relationship boundaries often disrupt long-standing patterns, norms, and expectations. They perpetuate because they likely benefit the other person. When you set a limit, it can feel abrupt or jarring, not because the boundary is wrong, but because it changes a dynamic that had previously gone unchecked. This is why we can be so quick to drop a boundary we set. We interpret the reaction as a reason to reverse course, when we should really see it as a sign that we made the right choice.

At their core, relationship boundaries protect your time, emotional energy, and roles from creeping beyond their edges. They help you recognize when you are carrying responsibilities that aren't yours to hold. This is where boundaries are often misunderstood: they aren't acts of rejection, control, or punishment. Relationship boundaries are simply information. They clarify what you can offer, what you can't, and how you're willing to engage.

Relationship boundaries teach people how to treat you. They establish rules of engagement for how you'll interact, not to create distance but to make connections more sustainable. Clear, kind boundaries don't damage relationships; they protect them from resentment, burnout, and unspoken expectations. A well-stated and carefully upheld boundary reduces confusion and enhances trust.

If the people-pleaser in you is still a little leery of this, you're not alone. Deep inside my psyche lives a delightful Nazarene grandma who is impeccably dressed, believes hospitality is non-negotiable, and insists that Jell-O is a salad (and for that, she is absolutely correct, don't come for my Jell-O salads). She maintains that a good woman keeps everyone comfortable and well-fed, and she is willing to put herself last every time.

My mother's surprise that boundaries can be a 'thing' likely came from this very same place, and it is a cycle that can be hard to break. With time and practice, I've come to understand that boundaries aren't the opposite of kindness; they are actually kindness in action. They create clarity. They reduce resentment. They help relationships flourish rather than fracture.

A few years ago, my son got a real-life example of how boundaries create clarity. Our neighborhood has about thirty houses and roughly thirty children, meaning we had a lot of new relationships to navigate when we first moved in. I love having a house full of kids and knowing that mine are under my roof brings a lot of peace. But there is absolutely a limit to how much chaos we can absorb. So, after a few months of living with a revolving door of small visitors, I set a reasonable household boundary for having neighbors over: not every night and not when we're not home.

My son pushed back on this, saying, "But Mom! They're going to think we're not *nice!*" And because I am my grandmother's granddaughter, I felt that. But I told him, gently, "Let's focus on being *kind*, not just nice. Kindness is showing people exactly how we expect to be treated, and how we will treat them back."

A few days later, my kids went to their grandparents' house for fall break, and we learned a lesson in boundary-setting. That first day, I was also away from the house, but my smartwatch kept going off. The doorbell was pinging my watch nonstop. *Ding dong, ding dong, ding freakin' dong.* It was like all other activities were suspended on my watch that day, no texts or reminders, just faces popping up on the doorbell. I seriously wondered if the doorbell camera had possessed my watch.

One kid after another would ring the doorbell, sometimes several kids at once. Maybe they thought that if they sent the smallest sibling first and then the oldest, it would have a different result than the first *ding dong.* But the tall and small ding dongs had the same result: there was no one home.

When I pulled into my driveway that night, the whole crew of kids mobbed my car, peering in the windows with a feral, *Lord of the Flies* energy. As I exited the car, they called to me, all speaking as one entity, all their voices mixing together into an otherworldly sound: "*WHERE'S PORTER?!*"

Juggling the four bags and three beverages I was extracting from my car, I said, "Guys, he's at his grandparents' house, and he'll be gone until Wednesday." Before I even had the words out of my mouth, they turned and ran off.

And do you know what didn't happen until Wednesday?

My doorbell didn't ring. My watch was so quiet I wondered if it was still working. The silence continued over the next few days, and while it was a welcome change, I started missing all the kids. When I pulled into the neighborhood that Wednesday night, I found my son surrounded by his neighbor friends, happily playing in the street. They weren't upset with him. They were just glad he was back.

Remember the feeling of anticipation just before you rang a friend's doorbell when you were young? And the corresponding let down when no one was home? Boundaries signal to the other person, "I won't be available," so they know not to get their hopes up. We're saying, "Here's exactly what you can expect from me, and you can expect me to deliver on that." It's clear. It's consistent. It's kind.

I shared this story with my son in the context of boundary setting, explaining to him the impact of setting and upholding the expectation. I reminded him of the limits I wanted to set, and how this was a perfect example of clarity creating kindness. He agreed, and we agreed on "not every night, not when we're not home."

When I surveyed how people got out of burnout, boundaries were mentioned over and over. Several mentioned being aware of their energy drains and the impact of saying 'yes' to too many things. One person responded: "Setting boundaries - with others and with myself - is a big help. I've also become much more comfortable with saying 'no,' and with cancelling or changing plans without guilt or shame if the situation no longer works for me."

This response is perfection, no notes. Understanding that boundaries are for yourself and others; saying no; and ditching the guilt: check, check, and check.

Relationship Boundaries in Real Life

Boundaries don't always have to be perfectly crafted or overly rehearsed. In fact, I think the simpler the boundary, the more likely it is to be respected. Sometimes boundaries sound like curiosity. Asking, "what have you tried?" is the nicer way of saying, "Have you asked the Googles?" Sometimes a boundary is a pause, telling someone, "Let's revisit this tomorrow." Translation: I do not do on-demand emotional labor.

People gravitate towards others who are happy to help, but that can cause all kinds of problems. Redirection can aid you if you are always the go-to. This might sound like saying, "Jim is the project manager; he's your guy." It is still kind and doesn't steal your time and energy. Silence is also a boundary. Refusing to respond to a demanding text from a family member or not immediately responding to an email marked "urgent" can conserve your energy. When everything is urgent and important, nothing is important.

My favorite boundary is one word: "No." If your Southern upbringing requires a softer landing, it might sound like "No, thank you." Either way, declining the invitation, the drama, or the demand is a very effective relationship boundary.

Now that you have established boundaries with other people, it's time to tackle what may be one of your biggest adversaries: yourself. The good news is that if you're having a hard time setting relationship boundaries, working on your internal boundaries can help you find your ground, making the practice of setting boundaries with yourself even more vital to your escape from quicksand.

SOLID GROUND

Boundaries & Relationship Boundaries

Orientation: Your Relationship with Boundaries

1. When you hear the word *boundaries*, what comes to mind first? Is there a specific person, situation, or feeling that immediately comes to mind?

2. What beliefs or assumptions have shaped how you think about boundaries? Which of those messages still creates a mental block for you today?

Relationship Boundaries

1. Where are you feeling resentment, tension, or emotional distance from others right now? What feelings might be underneath that reaction: fatigue, disappointment, overwhelm, grief?

2. What boundaries in relationships would help you regain time or energy? What feels unsustainable if nothing changes?

3. What boundary is trying to emerge here? If helpful, draft it using curiosity, a pause, or redirection. This does not need to be perfect or ready to use, just be honest and give it a try.

CHAPTER 5

Resilience is Your Resistance

Whereas relationship boundaries protect us from others, resilience boundaries protect us from our own habits: people-pleasing, perfectionism, overcommitting, and martyrdom (favorite hobbies of quicksand dwellers everywhere). Resilience boundaries are the internal agreements you make about how you speak to yourself, what you prioritize, and how you spend and manage your energy. They include self-talk, discipline, consistency, and the promises you make and keep to yourself.

Essentially, resilience boundaries are just like relationship boundaries, only the relationship is with yourself. These are complicated because we don't always treat ourselves with the same kindness and respect that we give others. We can push ourselves harder and further because surely, we can willpower our way out of everything. If this sounds very familiar to you, trust that I'm not reading your emails, I have just been there too.

We push the boundaries of resilience by saying yes to everyone and everything, but not to ourselves or our margin. Defaulting to worst-case-scenario catastrophizing erodes resilience. The late-night mental run-throughs of all the what-ifs can break the relationship with your resolve. Every time you choose productivity at all costs over rest or feeling your feelings, you teach your body and brain that you are an unreliable narrator, and you sink further into the quicksand.

Relationship boundaries are hard to set. Resilience boundaries are hard to honor. These are often the first boundaries to be compromised when life gets busy: sleep, hydration, a morning routine, a promise to take a break, a commitment to stop working at a certain time, a practice ground you. Because these boundaries are internal, no one else notices when you break them.

But you do. Just like relationship boundaries teach others how to treat you, resilience boundaries teach you to treat yourself the way you deserve to be treated. If the Parks and Rec "Treat yo'self" sequence just came to your mind, good. That's exactly what you need to do: treat yourself with kindness and maybe a few indulgences here and there.

Remember the commercials that showed an egg representing your brain, then a cracked egg, and told you, "This is your brain on drugs."? Yes, another '80s baby reference. I probably should have called this book Millennial Memories, but I digress. Your brain in quicksand is like that: scrambled, messy, and a little untrustworthy. When you are in quicksand, burned out and exhausted from trying to escape, you probably aren't saying many kind things to yourself. Your brain is telling you that you are not enough and to keep trying harder.

But we know from all those '80s movies and shows that what we need is slow, steady, and sustainable movement. We need messages that tell us we are good enough, we've got this, and that our hair still looks nice even when it's covered in mud. And because spelunking in quicksand is a solo sport, it is up to you to say kind things to yourself. All that negative self-talk is counterproductive to your ascent into the daylight, and you need to treat yo' self with kind words of validation.

When you're in quicksand, resilience boundaries matter more than ever. They help prevent you from slipping back into the patterns that sent you under in the first place. Even keeping the smallest promises to yourself rebuilds trust, and that trust becomes fuel. It stabilizes you. It strengthens your footing and empowers you to hold the relationship boundaries that once felt impossible.

These self-boundaries provide you with the protection you need to sustain your journey out of the quicksand. As you set and uphold these boundaries and regain self-trust, you begin to recognize when you need them before you've gone too far. This looks like taking a break when necessary, not waiting until you reach your breaking point. It means you learn to pay attention when something feels off, and connecting with that feeling helps you know what you need in that moment.

Resilience Boundaries in Real Life

Real-life resilience can look like setting limits on how long you ruminate on something. What's done is done, and what you need now is self-kindness. Maybe it's making a decision and sticking to it. I often find that when we hesitate, it's because we're afraid of hurting others' feelings or because we worry about how we will "look" to someone else. Embracing resilience boundaries looks like focusing on making yourself happy rather than worrying about pleasing everyone else. Boundaries will help you feel comfortable with making yourself comfortable. I am fairly certain it is impossible to please *everyone*, so worry about yourself and let the rest go.

Resilience shows up by honoring the commitments you made

to yourself. Someone will always need you, and it's right when you scheduled time to go to the gym or take a walk. Where possible, hold that commitment and take care of yourself.

I used to think that taking time for myself, whether it was for a workout, dinner with a friend, or something "extra," was selfish or self-indulgent. As a working mom and wife, I felt that anything that didn't serve someone else was frivolous. Once I realized that taking time for myself made me better at all my roles, I flipped the script to call out that these are necessary for my mental health and overall happiness.

On the flip side, there will be times when you are tired or just need a break, and you decide to skip that workout. Resilience involves listening to your gut and being kind to yourself about whatever choice you make. Sometimes self-discipline can be pushed to the extreme, and by powering through when you really need rest, you can do more harm than good. Discipline without self-awareness can turn into self-punishment. When we let shame motivate us or fear that rest makes us undisciplined or lazy, we ignore every warning light and push through the check engine lights that are screaming at us.

It took me a long time to learn that I didn't have to be perfect with my commitments to be good. If I missed a workout class, I could pick up the next one, and no one would be standing at the door calling me out for missing the last one. It turns out I was my worst bully, and I needed to be kinder to myself.

Hustle & Float

I also know that some seasons in life don't allow us any kindness. With two kids in different schools, the final rush of each school semester brings events, volunteer shifts, and other schedule disruptions that make May and December hectic. May brings the delight of dueling conference seasons for my husband and me, creating an impressive game of schedule Tetris. Naturally, Mother's Day is also in May and we are expected to pause it all for a day to relax and enjoy. December, of course, sees May and raises it with holidays, gifting, and freezing temperatures.

I saw something on Instagram that changed how I set my resilience boundaries during these seasons. They called it hustle and float. If you've ever been rafting, you know that sometimes you have to be ready to hustle. When the rapids come, you push yourself almost to the limit to get through the turbulent waters. But you only have the energy to hustle if you follow up with float time to rest and recover.

Knowing that the end of the school and calendar years will try to capsize me, I have learned to protect my schedule accordingly. I reserve those "hustle weeks" to remind my brain that, unless a big client requests me, I am generally unavailable for any additional work, meetups, events, or other distractions.

Of course, over the last two Mays, my biggest client came calling, and I, of course, answered. This meant more than your average end-of-school-year juggling and asking my husband, our parents, and babysitters for extra help. Last year, we had an impressive three days that included the last day of school, my biggest speaking engagement, and a family wedding out of state, where my daughter was the flower girl. None of these commitments were eligible for us to decline. I immediately recognized this as extreme hustle time, so I built in non-negotiable float time in the form of a family getaway to force myself to pause.

It took top-notch organization, many lists, and an impressive packing system, but I went from the client engagement to the family wedding straight to a cabin on the river. The kind of place where the only things on the agenda are sleeping late, drinking coffee on the porch, and eating your body weight in s'mores. I knew this was the only way I would relax after so much hustling, and it was exactly what we all needed. The old me would have gone straight home, unpacked my bag immediately, and jumped back into the daily grind. The post-quicksand version of me knew that I needed to reset my system first.

If you're like me and wired to push yourself to the very end, it might take some time to get used to downtime. December and May may not be as hectic for you. You might have different seasons that choose violence. But know what they are, then make sure to build in float time. You may need to start slow, maybe with a nap or some self-care like a massage.

A friend of mine has three kids with birthdays back-to-back, so her husband started scheduling a massage for her every year immediately after the third birthday party (round of applause for this spouse, please). When you start to recognize the seasons when you push, you can begin to hardwire times to pull back.

Upholding promises to yourself teaches your mind and body that you are trustworthy, an essential stepping-stone on the path out of quicksand. If you are looking for someone to save you from yourself, I have to tell you that no one is coming. The call is coming from inside the house, and it is up to you to answer. Stop working when you said you would, set a timer if you need help keeping your promise. Block the apps on your phone so you aren't scrolling long after you should be sleeping. Your nervous system needs consistency, and that comes from you upholding the boundaries you promised it.

As you honor these commitments, you might physically feel your body relax. Resilience boundaries aren't just abstract; they are somatic. Check in with yourself and reflect on how you feel after a walking break or when you take time to relax after a busy week. Over time, honoring these small commitments to yourself sends a message that you are tuned in, paying attention, and ready to listen. You begin to repair those broken connections, which in turn allows you to hear even more.

This self-trust creates the foundation for other types of boundaries. When you are kind to yourself, relationship boundaries become natural rather than feel forced. When you improve the direct line to your needs, decisions take less energy. You stop needing external validation to justify your needs, making rest and recovery non-negotiable rather than subject to negotiation. Over time, this follow-through becomes second nature, and you'll realize you have rebuilt the relationship with yourself through self-kindness and self-trust.

I also know that sometimes you're hustling so hard in the quicksand that basic tasks like showering, making food, or scheduling a doctor's appointment feel impossible. When you feel that way, the internal work feels Herculean. I've been there, but I found my way out, and you can too. That's where renewal boundaries finish out the return to connection.

SOLID GROUND

Resilience Boundaries (Boundaries with Yourself)

1. When do you notice feeling disconnected from yourself? When and how do you tend to deprioritize your own needs?

2. What does your self-talk sound like when you are tired, overwhelmed, or behind?

3. Which promises to yourself do you find most important to keep?

4. Where might you need clearer boundaries for your time, energy, or expectations of yourself?

5. What might rebuilding trust with yourself look like, one small step at a time?

6. When are times you need to build in float time after a hustle?

CHAPTER 6

Listen to the Whispers

Renewal boundaries are those you know you need, but they often get moved to the back burner when you are overwhelmed or under pressure. Nearly everything in the "health" category falls here: mental, physical, spiritual, and emotional. When we sink into quicksand, renewal can fall off the radar altogether. When I was descending in quicksand, I ignored my physical health for far too long. I postponed appointments, skipped workouts, sacrificed sleep, and replaced meals with caffeine. I was a walking example of deferred maintenance. Quicksand convinces you that caring for yourself is indulgent, irresponsible, or optional.

One thing I know to be true: You get one body for this one wild and beautiful life, and it deserves care. Renewal boundaries protect the habits and resources that restore you. They include medical appointments, therapy, movement, hydration, and nourishment. Not as punishment, nor as another item on the to-do list, but as essential maintenance for the life you want to live.

Listen to the Whispers

When I was COO, I would wake up with a watering right eye. I would get it to stop watering so I could put on eye makeup (because priorities), and then I would go to work. I was the conductor keeping the unwieldy train on the track during a global pandemic, after all.

Months passed, and my right eye kept watering. Always just that one. Every morning, I'd wake up, and my eye would water enough to be annoying. I remember telling my husband, "It feels like I have this not quite a grain of rice, but almost, in there. It just feels weird." On more than one occasion, he reminded me to make an appointment.

But I was really busy. I was running a healthcare organization while the world was falling apart around us. I didn't have time to get in my car, drive across town, and sit in the eye doctor's office. So I just let it water. It was fine.

Until it wasn't.

One morning, I woke up in terrible pain. It was the same day I was supposed to meet my new boss, the leader of the organization acquiring my company. Why wouldn't it be? I scheduled a virtual appointment to get some drops because I convinced the doctor on the screen that it was pink eye (ew, but fixable) and worked from home the rest of the day.

You probably think that I didn't go to that dinner with my new boss. But, oh, dear reader, you would be wrong. Instead, we just changed the arrangement at the table so that my good eye was facing him. The restaurant was dark, it was *fine.* But you and I both know now, that *it wasn't fine.* Let's be honest, I knew then that it wasn't fine, but I didn't want to miss out on my literal seat at the table.

The morning after dinner, my boss Jeff said, "Call your eye doctor or I will call mine, but you are going to get seen today!" One of my teammates had to drive me because I wasn't safe to drive with only one good eye. Note that I showed up to work, but I wasn't fit to drive. Turns out, I had a torn cornea. I was given some numbing drops and a contact lens to serve as a band-aid while my eye healed.

But my eye is as stubborn as I am, and it refused to heal. My cornea tore four more times over the next few years. In case you are wondering, it is extremely painful. Your eye turns a terrifying shade of red, and you have to wear a contact lens and use drops three times a day for as long as it takes to heal itself. Since that first incident, I've had four surgeries and literally dozens of hours in numerous doctors' offices to fix my "bad eye." The technical term for my bad eye is "recurrent corneal erosion," which sounds pretty on-brand for something you get when you are in quicksand.

I have so many stories about that eye, like the time I had to pay a babysitter $100 to drive 60 miles to bring me a contact lens because my cornea re-tore while we were on a lake trip with friends (trust that I always travel with a contact now). My husband once had to guide me through the eye doctor's office like my own personal seeing-eye human because it tore so completely that I temporarily lost my vision. The timing of my third eye surgery meant that I spent my 39th birthday wearing an eye patch in a dark room. You get the point. It was a less-than-delightful experience that ended up impacting me at less-than-optimal times.

If I had made an appointment with the doctor when my eye first started watering, there would be no story here to tell. My eye was watering to protect itself from ripping, but I wasn't doing anything to help it protect me. I could've avoided all of this if I had just gone to the doctor when I first noticed the issue. There is a saying, "Listen to your body when it whispers so you won't have to hear it scream." I tell the story of my eye, so maybe you will start listening to the whispers.

I would be willing to bet that many of you are putting off an appointment because you simply don't think you have the time to go. It is probably an -ologist. Maybe it is for your creaky knee, or the weird headaches you get after you read too long, or the spot on the back of your shoulder that your cousin pointed out to you. Whatever it is, please call and make the appointment. They'll probably offer something like "9:47 a.m., seven months and four days from now," and guess what? You can definitely make that work. No matter how much time it takes away from work or your life, it's worth it, as you'll get back by not putting it off as long as possible.

Move your body

When I was in the quicksand, I constantly put off exercise. I always thought that physical activity had to be a slog and it had to be painful to make an impact. When I began setting renewal boundaries, I realized I needed to change that paradigm.

I can't believe I've gone this far into the book without telling you about my love for Pilates. I've been practicing Pilates for three years, and I'm obsessed. But before I discovered Pilates, I didn't *know* what my body enjoyed. Exercise felt like a punishment, like a necessary evil. I didn't want to do it, so I didn't enjoy doing it, and I didn't prioritize it.

Once I found Pilates, it changed everything for me. I feel strong and capable after an hour of deep breathing and building core strength. When you're on a machine that looks like a medieval torture device, there are only so many things you can think about. For anyone who knows me well, it probably comes as no surprise that I fell in love with a very efficient exercise that checks a lot of boxes all at once.

Find movement that moves you. Keep trying new things until you discover something your body loves. A friend of mine realized in her late 30s that she loved hiking. Another friend recently started weightlifting to feel strong and keep up with her kids. Comedian JVN took up figure skating in their 30s, and while they look great doing it, they won't be heading to the Olympics, and that is okay!

That also busts another exercise myth for me: you don't have to be the best at it to keep doing it. My perfectionist, people-pleaser brain once thought I had to be the best in the class to keep it up. But now that I see exercise as something that brings me joy and fulfillment, I don't care what anyone else thinks about my form or my abilities. As it turns out, no one cares if you're good at it or not; they are focused on themselves.

Sleep Over All Else

Our physical health is vital, and sleep is probably the most important thing you can do for your body. I used to consider sleep in the category of a necessary evil, like exercise, simply a box to check, until I received a reality check.

I used to have a lovely doctor, but getting an appointment was hard, and when I did finally get in, he was rushed. I didn't feel like I was getting the help I needed. When I eventually got over the worry that I would be hurting his feelings, I changed doctors. Did you know that you're an adult and you can just change doctors? And that you don't have to wonder forever if they hate you now? They don't, so find a doctor that you like and let the old one go in peace.

When I saw my new doctor, I sat down in her office and immediately overshared everything I was doing wrong. I drank too much. I needed to lose weight. I didn't work out enough. Also, maybe I felt like I was losing my mind? She ignored all of that (for the time being; we did eventually circle back on the losing my mind part), and she gently asked about my sleep. Did I feel like I was getting enough? Did I sleep well?

I laughed and told her I had gotten SO much better at that, and I was up to sleeping about five hours a night. She tried to keep her chill but failed and told me firmly, "Until you get your sleep under control, I don't care about any of the rest of that. 'Sleep over all else' is your new motto."

Sleep and I have a very odd relationship. I can sleep anywhere, anytime, except in my bed at night. Planes? Check. Trains? Check. Automobiles? Check, even after drinking a full cup of coffee (but always when I am a passenger, I promise). I am an A+ napper. The sad truth behind all these impressive facts is that I can only do this because nighttime sleep often eludes me, and I am almost always in a sleep deficit.

When my doctor advised me to get more sleep, I downloaded an app that tracks my sleep and shows me how far I am in the hole each day. I discovered that I was over 10 hours behind. The app assigns an energy potential percentage, and I was operating at 30-40%. How does this happen to a Champion Sleeper? Because I can lie down to sleep at night, only to see every hour on the clock pass me by in a bout of insomnia.

One of my earliest memories—and a story that Jay loved to tell about me—was when I was four years old. He got up in the middle of the night to find me sitting on the couch. Concerned, he asked, "Are you having trouble sleeping?" and I replied, "Yes, it is just that when I close my eyes, I play back the movie of my day and think of all the things I could have done better." At four years old, y'all. Proof that both my insomnia and perfectionist tendencies were woven into my DNA.

But the version of me emerging from quicksand prioritizes sleep. I uphold my commitment to renewal by setting resilience boundaries to hold myself accountable. I listen to my body and go to sleep when it tells me I am tired. I ask my husband for weekend mornings to sleep in to reduce my sleep debt. I take naps when I know I need to, even if it is just 15 minutes. I wish I could say I find my way to bed earlier, but as a lifelong night owl, I fear that may actually require a lobotomy.

Our bodies need sleep to recover. Getting out of the quicksand is exhausting, and you'll need to be well-rested. Sleep serves as the ultimate renewal boundary since that's its actual job: renewing your energy and resilience for the work of getting out of the quicksand.

Mental Health Matters

I've always supported people in therapy, but for a long time, I did not think that was part of my path. My worker-bee tendencies didn't imagine a reality where I could leave my desk, drive across town, cry off my eye makeup, and return to work. That all changed during our mid-pandemic house move (reminder: zero stars, do not recommend).

I was finally tackling my new closet when my husband found me crying in a tangled pile of swimsuits and party dresses. Through sobs, I exclaimed, "We will never travel again! We will never go to a party again!" The pandemic was especially rough on those of us with off-the-charts extroversion. My sweet husband, the one who looked at approximately 400 houses to find *the* one with *the* closet that I was now crying in, said the kindest thing anyone can say to someone in that situation: "Maybe you should talk to someone."

I followed his advice and found someone experienced with my specific mental health needs who was accepting new patients, took my insurance, and offered virtual visits. We began our relationship in the summer of 2020, and to this day, I have never shared oxygen with my therapist. One time I was running late for a session (yes, I can even run late getting upstairs, it is a talent), and my husband said, "Don't worry about brushing your teeth, she can't smell your breath!" He was right: She meets me, quite literally, where I am.

Let's talk for a minute about how to find a professional when you are ready to take this step. As a recovering HR Professional, I want to share a quick aside about your options. Most full-time, benefit-eligible employees have access to some form of employee assistance program. It's probably the most under-utilized benefit there is. Employee Assistance Programs (EAP) are voluntary, confidential programs that offer assessments, referrals, and follow-up services for your mental health.

When you're phenomenally burned out and don't know where to start, thinking about finding a mental health provider can feel daunting. An EAP handles the legwork for you. Typically, you get multiple visits each year; you don't have to worry about what insurance they accept, or whether they are accepting new patients. All of those logistics are handled, and you can just start talking to someone.

In addition, more employers are providing mental health benefits. If you would prefer a more long-term relationship with someone (and I highly recommend that route), then take steps to find someone. The EAP can serve as a stopgap until you have the energy to tackle finding a provider who fits your needs. I do suggest you brush your teeth for them if you are meeting in person, though. That's a boundary I don't recommend skipping.

I am so grateful that I had already established this relationship with my therapist prior to losing my brother. I truly don't know how I would have made it through my grief without the guidance she provides. By the time I lost Jay, she already knew how close I was to my family, how important he was to me, and how hard it was to watch him get sick so fast.

There was no playing catch-up. She already knew me and how his presence shaped my life. As an established patient, she was able to get me in quickly when I needed to talk.

I will be forever grateful for each hour I get with my therapist, but sometimes we need a little more help than just a sounding board to listen and provide insight.

I have two degrees in psychology (which I am sure makes me a delightful patient), but I always shied away from antidepressants. I always saw them as some big horse pill that would dull me, take away part of my personality, or dampen my spirit. Once I understood my complicated relationship with grief, I thought medication would quash my ability to grieve, to hear my brother's voice.

I was scrolling through Instagram one day and saw a post from Sara Bareilles (whom I love but didn't actually follow), and she had the smallest pill in her open hand. Beneath the photo was a post about how the medication she was on changed her life.

As I continued walking through my grief, I kept thinking about that post. About that tiny pill. It was smaller than my daily allergy medicine. To think that such a tiny pill could help with my depression blew my mind. I bookmarked that post and went back to it several times, like a lifeline or a beacon of hope.

At my next doctor's appointment, I mentioned that talk therapy was helping, but I was still struggling with my mental health. She gave me a self-assessment to complete. After she reviewed my answers, we discussed my symptoms and options for medication. The same doctor who helped rewire my relationship with sleep also helped me rewire my relationship with my brain and pharmaceuticals.

A few months after I started my medication, I was out to lunch with a friend, talking about the mental load of motherhood, work, and everything we were each juggling. I mentioned my new medication a little sheepishly, and she quickly replied, "You know, if your brain doesn't make the right chemicals, store-bought is fine!" It was a perfect explanation of what I needed and why it was okay. I think of her anecdote often.

Looking back, I have no doubt that Jay has been (and still is) sending me messages through music, movies, TV shows, and Instagram posts (even though he called Instagram "QVC for millennials"). I know that Sara Bareilles's post appeared on my feed for a reason.

Our bodies and brains aren't wired for the world we live in today. The onslaught of information, notifications, and sadness from all over the world being beamed into the palm of your hand all the time is too much for our little cerebellums that were meant to eat berries in a cave by a peaceful river.

Renewal boundaries like therapy ensure our brains are equipped to handle the climb out of the quicksand. Medication can help bolster those efforts, even if only temporarily. Exercise and caring for our bodies and minds become our superpower. Prioritizing renewal can help propel you forward and onto solid ground.

SOLID GROUND

Renewal Boundaries (Health & Capacity)

1. Are there physical or mental health needs you've been putting off or minimizing? What could your body be asking for that you haven't slowed down enough to hear?

2. How is your sleep right now, on a scale of 1–10? What would it take to boost that score by just one point?

3. What movement, rest, or care are you curious about exploring, not because you *should*, but because it feels supportive?

4. How is your mental health at the moment? What kind of support would help you feel more equipped? (Professional, relational, or practical)

5. How might honoring these boundaries protect your energy, health, or relationships? What could become possible if you stopped negotiating with your own limits?

CHAPTER 7

The C^3 Checklist

Setting relationship, resilience, or renewal boundaries can be challenging. If they feel like they're not working, it's usually because one of these three pieces is missing: Are you being clear, concise, and consistent? The 3 Cs (Clear, Concise, Consistent) give you a way to check your footing and course-correct in real time.

Be Clear

Clarity is the foundation of every boundary. You need to name what you're saying *yes* to, what you're saying *no* to, and what you're no longer willing to carry. Maybe you're saying no to rescuing a coworker who missed their deadline. Maybe you're saying yes to time with friends, rest, or a moment to think. When you articulate the boundary clearly, you remove the ambiguity that causes conflict and resentment. Everyone knows what you're protecting and why it matters.

Be Concise

This is the step most people struggle with. I include myself in this because all my thoughts come out into the universe. We think boundaries require justification, apology, or negotiation, but those extra sentences are usually just fear dressed up as politeness. You don't need a monologue. You don't need to soften the landing. You don't need to twist yourself into a pretzel to make it palatable. You just need to speak it into the universe.

Just like authenticity, only you can give yourself permission to advocate for what you need. Long explanations dilute your authority, and apologies undermine the clarity you just worked so hard to establish. Boundaries should be spoken clearly and with conviction, not with regret.

A clear boundary might sound like:

"I can't take that on."

"That timeline won't work for me."

"I'm not available, but here's what I can offer."

Boundaries should be short, respectful, and to the point. Notice it isn't short and sweet, just clear and kind. That is one of the hardest things for me to get used to, so be prepared that it may take some practice.

Be Consistent

Consistency is where boundaries either take root or fall apart. A boundary is only as strong as your willingness to uphold it, especially when someone pushes back. And people *will* push back. They may get frustrated, confused, or disappointed. That's not a sign you're doing it wrong. It's a sign that the dynamic is shifting. It is not your job to manage someone else's feelings about your boundary. It *is* your job to honor the line you drew.

And here's the secret: the toughest person to stay consistent with is usually yourself. It's easy to slip back into old patterns, say yes automatically, or let an internal boundary dissolve under stress. That's why you need systems that support consistency: reminders, accountability partners, scripts, routines, or even a simple question you ask yourself: *"Does this align with my values and energy right now?"*

Consistency turns boundaries from a momentary decision into a long-term practice. It strengthens your resilience, protects your renewal, and keeps you from drifting back toward burnout.

Stepping Onto Solid Ground

Boundaries subtract. They remove obligation, resentment, overcommitment, exhaustion, and other people's expectations. They lighten the weight that burnout piles on your chest. They erase the guilt that sometimes accompanies caring for your physical and mental health. But that subtraction gives you freedom, room to breathe, and the capacity you need to get out of the quicksand. Boundaries aren't walls. They're paths that lead out of the quicksand. When you set boundaries in your relationships, with yourself, and for your health, you create the stability you need for the final piece of your recovery: counterbalance.

SOLID GROUND

The C³ Checklist

Use this quick reference anytime you're unsure whether a boundary is well-formed.

Clear

- Is the boundary specific and easy to understand?
- Does it name what will or won't happen?

Concise

- Can it be said simply, without over-explaining or justifying?
- Does it eliminate unnecessary details or excuses?

Consistent

- Are you willing to reinforce it if necessary?
- Do your actions match what you've communicated?

If the answer is "no" to any of these, revisit, refine, and try again.

CHAPTER 8

Confessions of a Flipped Stroller

"I had an internal belief that there was surely a way to get it all done. I just hadn't figured it out yet."

When my daughter Vivian was six months old, my sister and I flew to California to visit our brother. I was still nursing, so my daughter came along. I had never flown with her without my husband there to help, so my sister stepped in. A moment of appreciation for my sister: there has never been a time when I needed her that she didn't show up, sometimes even without me asking. When she shows up, she usually has snacks and a purse-sized emergency kit filled with things you didn't even realize you needed.

This particular time, her support looked like waiting for me at check-in and helping me through security with the stroller, car seat, and massive diaper bag so I could focus on my daughter. Once we got through security, we celebrated by buying giant coffees that we nestled into the stroller's cup holders. To free up my hands, I used an industrial-strength carabiner to hook the diaper bag to the back of the stroller, just below the coffee cups.

Once we wheeled our way to the gate and got settled, my sister walked away to go to the restroom. The moment she walked away, my daughter started to cry, so I lifted her out of her stroller. In doing so, the entire stroller (sans baby!) flipped over backwards, causing those brand-new coffees to spill into the overpacked diaper bag.

It is worth reminding you that I was holding my daughter so she was safe, but I was still in a full-on panic. I placed her in the big airport chairs, blocking her from falling through the armrest opening with one leg while simultaneously trying to flip the stroller back over. I was sweating profusely as I stood one-legged and frazzled. I was stringing along an impressive list of curse words not so much under, but just over, my breath. It was as charming as you are picturing in your mind.

I finally managed to get it upright and strapped her back into the stroller, just in time for my sister to return. She must have sensed a disturbance in the force and looked around like, "What did I miss?" I started laughing and recounted the story. She said, "I guess you forgot that Vivian was your counterbalance, keeping the stroller, the bag, and the coffees all upright."

Throughout our trip, the word "*counterbalance*" kept recurring in my mind. Work/life balance was something I had studied, researched, and presented on for years, but I had never found the answer. What even is work/life balance? Most of the research centers on separating the two, but we work at home, we do life at work, and I think trying to keep them separate is an exercise in futility.

The definition of counterbalance is literally a weight that balances another weight. When my sister used "counterbalance" to describe the comical stroller flip, I started to think of balance in a new light. What if we could balance both work and life on one side with something on the other side: a counterbalance? I considered what could go on the other side of the equation to help balance out everything we put into the overstuffed bag that is work and life.

As I reflected on the stroller story, I realized the three parts of counterbalance serve as the antidote to doubt, the final component of the quicksand. The feelings that we aren't good enough, questioning why we should even keep trying, and doubting that we will ever find our way out of the quicksand are what keep us stuck. If you are all the way in the muck, you are also disconnected from your sense of self and your community, making it nearly impossible to escape.

Life doesn't cut us a break just because we are in quicksand. Instead, the demands of work, life, and everything in between stack up, and the load we carry continues to grow. Doubt creeps in when we are carrying more than we can handle. We begin to wonder, rightfully so, if we can even begin to accomplish everything we set out to do. When the bag is overfilled, we need support to help keep everything in place, like Vivian was for me in the stroller.

That day at the airport, with a flipped stroller on the ground, I learned that we need to accept help, we can't overpack the bag, and we need to drink the coffee. Those same three lessons translate into: **Ease, Evaluate, Enjoy**. These steps aren't complicated, but they ask you to disrupt deeply ingrained patterns. ***Ease*** reminds us that asking for help isn't a sign of weakness; it provides additional strength to find our way to solid ground. When we ***evaluate***, we refocus on what matters most instead of agreeing to every opportunity that comes our way. ***Enjoy*** encourages us to make time for ourselves instead of always rushing to the next thing.

Counterbalance isn't about perfectly balancing everything; it's intentionally adding weights on the other side of the scale so life doesn't tip you over.

Ease

When the stroller flipped, everyone around me rushed to help: business travelers, fellow moms, families, all people who could clearly see I was in trouble. To each one I replied, "No thanks, I'm good." And by "good" I meant one leg in the air, the other balancing a baby in a too-big chair while sweating and cursing myself.

Why didn't I say yes? Maybe it was my fierce independence, maybe embarrassment, or maybe both. This idea of "I'm good" sounds a lot like when we are overwhelmed, and people offer to help, but we decline, doesn't it? We think we can do it better, easier, or faster than anyone else. We worry that if we let someone else do it, we won't be needed anymore. The stories you tell yourself are your ego talking. Your ego is an unreliable narrator. If we are ever going to get out of the quicksand, we have to be willing to not just take the help but ask for it too.

Ask for Help

Asking for help doesn't come easily to me. It feels like a sign of weakness, burdening others, or asking too much. But it's a skill that saved me from the quicksand, because I realized that my natural "do it myself" attitude was no longer serving me. If I wanted to find my way to solid ground, I needed some reinforcements.

For the last two decades, my husband has handled a lot of the visible things around the house. He's the grocery store-goer, meaning I can scarcely find my way around one anymore. He's the drop-off and pickup parent when he's in town, and I can scroll right past any meme about a man that can't find his way around the kitchen. But after twenty years together, our deep-rooted expectations around roles and responsibilities require revisiting. As it turns out, all that time doesn't grant you a magic portal into the other person's mind, so I have to speak up about what I need.

Often, my brain feels like a web browser with too many tabs. Not just any tabs, but busy ones with flashing lights and sounds. We created a running list on the counter called "tabs," where I write down the mental load tasks swirling in my brain. When he is in town, he reviews the list to see where he can help me close tabs. I no longer resent him for not knowing what's going on in my mind, and he knows how he can help me close tabs.

My other trick is to stretch out my empty hands and say, "I need you to take this." One time during the holiday overwhelm, I held out my hands and said, "Take this. It is all the Christmas presents we need to buy for your family." My to-do list was a mile long, and that task was a better fit for his knowledge and skills. Did he wait to shop until Christmas Eve? Yes. Did it get done? Also yes. Asking for help means releasing control, an exercise in discomfort that leads to relief.

Sometimes asking for help means reaching beyond your household: to siblings, parents, friends, neighbors, or coworkers. Be specific. People don't know how to help unless you tell them, but in my experience, they want to help you, especially in times of need. Sharing the load is a big step toward creating a counterbalance. It may be the hardest step for me, so be prepared that it might be for you too.

When in Doubt, Delegate

Delegation is simply transferring authority and responsibility for specific tasks to another person. When done well, it saves time, develops others, and ensures more than one person knows how to do the task. When delegation is done poorly or not at all, it becomes micromanagement. While micromanaging isn't part of my values, my tight control over some tasks has put me dangerously close to that label.

My best delegation story is so old it's practically a teenager, but it's too good not to share. Before my maternity leave with my son, I was planning out who would take on my tasks. One item I kept moving around was the monthly turnover report. It was a monster: three spreadsheets, each with seven to thirty-six tabs, and manually populated data that was combined into a report due by the 10th every month. I left it until the very last minute every month and assumed others would feel the same.

But I knew I had to allocate all my duties before I went on leave. So as my due date loomed, I waddled into our Payroll Coordinator's office. Sheepishly, I asked if she would mind taking over the report for the three months I would be out of the office. Her eyes lit up, and she said, "I thought you would never ask!"

I couldn't believe someone envied that task. As it turned out, she had been watching the report for years and had an idea to streamline the process and eliminate about 17 steps. She assumed I wouldn't want to give up something that went straight to leadership, so she never asked me about it.

Her skill set was a perfect fit for the report. She quickly learned the process and took charge just in time for my absence. An unexpected benefit was that by sending the report to the executive team and answering their questions, she was able to shine in front of leadership. Over time, they asked her to take on additional projects that further expanded her skill set. My least favorite task was her dream.

Are you guilty of holding onto things at work or at home that belong somewhere else too? What tasks do you dread or procrastinate because they are a misfit with your skills or preferences? Evaluate your to-do list under this lens and identify some things that can go elsewhere.

This is where it comes in handy to really know your people, both at work and at home. What are they interested in, what makes them tick, and what developmental opportunities might they enjoy? Obviously, in some scenarios, the list of who you can delegate tasks to is finite (until the dogs can take on chores, my list at home is 3 people, for example), but it is still worth taking stock of your tasks and asking if there is someone else who might be a better fit for items on your to-do list.

Outsource

My beloved hairstylist taught me one of my favorite sayings: "do what you do best and delegate the rest." I've listened to her and delegated all hair care to her. She has yet to steer me wrong, so I follow her advice here too. I am good at a few things and not good at a LOT, so it starts with knowing my strengths. As an entrepreneur, my time is literally my money (and I would argue that this is true of anyone), so I have to critically assess tasks that aren't a value-add for me to see whether they belong to someone or something else.

That 'something' might look like leaning on AI. I started asking Chat to write my meal plan and grocery list for the week, and it has saved me about an hour a week of begging everyone to tell me what they will eat. That little bit of relief from my (dinner) plate has made a difference, both in time and frustration.

Meal prep and planning services, grocery delivery, pickup, and automation fall under the category of outsourcing and can be a major time and frustration saver. I saw a story on Instagram about a mom who would order groceries online, then go to a yoga class while she waited for the pickup to be ready, then just tell her family she had gone to the grocery store. Genius! Hot take: yoga shouldn't need to be done in secret, but you do you.

Sometimes outsourcing is to someone. Disclaimer: I recognize that much of this section comes from a place of privilege, so no hard feelings if you skip it or judge me here. But if you are willing to stick with me, I will tell you that having a house helper has quite possibly saved my sanity, marriage, and maybe life.

A house helper is usually our babysitter, almost always a college student, and always a lifesaver. Most of my income and tuition money from ages 14 to 20 came from baby/house/pet-sitting, as well as running errands, so I see our hiring someone for a similar role as paying it forward in gratitude for all the wonderful people who trusted me with their children, homes, and furry friends along the way.

A few tasks that are perfectly suited for house helpers:

- Weekly laundry, folding, dishes, and kitchen cleaning
- Amazon returns
- Target or grocery pickup
- Switching out the seasons in kids' closets
- Addressing, stamping, and mailing invitations
- Teacher gifts, gift wrapping
- Dry cleaning, kid pickups, and dog pickups

If the fully-paid option is out of the question for you, think about creative ways you could still outsource. Is there a pre-teen in your neighborhood who could come play with your kids for a few hours or help you with projects around the house? Could you swap out with another mom to help each other tackle a few things? There are ways to get creative with this without overspending. The important part is that you at least consider it.

Evaluate

At the time of the stroller flip, I was a doomsday prepper when it came to packing. I have since reformed and now travel with a carry-on (yes, I do feel the need to brag). But that day, I had checked a giant suitcase, and my diaper bag/carry-on contained a month's worth of snacks, diapers, and outfits for four hours of travel. It was the sheer weight of that thing that caused the fast and dramatic flip.

If we are going to find counterbalance, we can't overpack the proverbial bag that is our calendar. Just like we discussed in the boundaries section, we have to lighten our load to make room for what matters most. Implementing boundaries is the first step; being consistent with how we structure our days lays the foundation for counterbalance. Each yes is a no to something else. A yes to an event is often a no to family time, joy, rest, or yourself. We must become more mindful about where we make commitments.

This starts by being clear about your values, both your own and your family's. Revisit your core values from the Authenticity chapter and identify your family's shared ones. Once you can articulate them, you can check your commitments against your values.

For our family, three things are non-negotiable: spring break travel, family dinners, and spending as many evenings at home as possible. Naming just those three things means that we do something every spring break (even if it is just a quick weekend getaway); we sit down to dinner as a family as many nights as possible (plus with a neighbor or two some nights); and we are selective about where we spend our time. It sounds simple, but articulating what matters most to our family creates a rubric that means that we have a jumpstart on carving out time for our family.

You might start by reviewing how you and your family spent your time last month and asking a few questions:

- Did your calendar reflect your values?
- What did you say yes to that you didn't want to do?
- What brought you joy?
- What drained you?

It also helps to identify what *isn't* on your calendar, but takes a lot of time. Hint: it's probably your phone. Our phones promise comfort and deliver chaos. We work and play in the same space, and it is so easy to let our phones dictate where we spend our time. To keep that from happening, I set limits on games, shopping, and social media when I need accountability. I have apps that help me stay accountable and focused on what matters.

Enjoy

The stroller incident shouldn't have been a big deal. The urgency came from the full cups of hot coffee pouring into the diaper bag. Had we sipped even a little or held them in our hands to enjoy, the whole thing would've been a blip. The same is true in our lives: the things that bring us joy are often the first things we set down "for later," only to find later never comes. Joy isn't optional.

The entire reason my sister and I flew to California was that our brother had just been diagnosed with leukemia, and we all wanted to be together. When we finally made it to him, one of our first questions was whether he had any idea that he was sick before the diagnosis. The only thing he could point to was a moment standing in his closet nearly two years earlier, feeling exhausted and thinking he couldn't remember a time when he had ever been so tired. What he chalked up to the tiredness of a busy executive climbing the ladder was actually the beginning of the illness that took his life.

His realization will stay with me for the rest of my life. My friends, we get one chance. One wild and beautiful life. It wasn't meant to be spent on Zoom or in boardrooms or chasing spotless houses. Enjoying your life isn't indulgent. The counterbalance is what keeps you alive. When we are in the quicksand, joy might seem like a luxury, but you need to think of it as a lifeline.

Drink the Coffee

Maybe you *do* actually drink your morning coffee. But are you pursuing the things that bring you joy? When you've done all the work that got you to this point, it's time to reclaim your joy and meaning. To reconnect with what makes you feel alive, let delight back in and remember that you can choose to do what you want, not just things that are productive. It's the difference between leaving the coffee in the cupholder and drinking it.

My longtime mentor has a framework for joy: One thing each day, one thing each week, one thing each month, and one thing each year. This might look like:

- Reading for 15 minutes on your back porch every day
- Calling your best friend once a week
- Scheduling a monthly massage
- Taking a trip every year

These little routines give you something to look forward to and also create structure and predictability, two things that can help get you out of the quicksand.

We can also find small moments of joy in our days if we pause long enough to appreciate them. Use the good pen, burn the nice candle, embarrass your kids in the drop-off line by belting your favorite '90s tune (bonus points if you do the dance moves). Music has brought me so much joy as I've moved on my way out of the quicksand. Concerts, playlists, and car karaoke have played a surprisingly large part of my recovery.

My sister discovered she loves to watercolor and carves out time for it whenever possible, even traveling with a setup to use whenever the moment strikes on a family trip. She has really developed a talent. I, however, am still using the kids' painting kit. And that's okay, I don't need to be good at it to join her when we travel together or watch the kids play in the backyard. Just a reminder: you don't have to be good at something to enjoy it.

Your worth is not contingent on your productivity. Ease the load. Evaluate what stays. Enjoy what delights you. These three steps do not clear your schedule, fix your inbox, or magically give you more hours in the day. What they do is release you from the doubt that makes you feel like you can't make your way to the surface. They give you a way out of the quicksand, back to yourself, and onto solid ground.

SOLID GROUND

Counterbalance

Orientation: Noticing the Imbalance

1. What feels unsustainable or out of balance right now? Where are you carrying too much, overextending yourself, or quietly letting doubt creep back in?

Ease: Letting Go of What Doesn't Belong to You

1. What are you holding onto that might no longer belong to you? Which responsibilities, expectations, or roles could be released, shared, or simplified?

2. Where might someone else actually be a better fit? What could you delegate, reassign, or stop doing altogether? What's stopping you?

3. If you could wave a magic wand to eliminate one chore, task, or responsibility, what would you choose? What does that answer reveal to you about what drains you most?

4. How do you feel about outsourcing or asking for help? What messages have you internalized about doing it all yourself? Is there support you know you need but don't know how to ask for?

Evaluate: Aligning Time With What Matters

1. What values matter most to you right now, both personally and as a family? Have they shifted over time?

2. When you look at your calendar or a typical week, does the way you spend your time reflect what you say you value? Where is there alignment, and where is there friction?

3. What are your non-negotiables? What commitments, rhythms, or boundaries help you decide what gets a yes and what gets a no?

4. Where are your time drains or quiet distractions (such as your phone, other people's urgency, habits that no longer serve you)? What would it look like to be more intentional in those areas?

Enjoy: Making Room for Joy

1. What have you been told about joy? Maybe that joy is selfish, indulgent, or only earned only after productivity?

2. How can you pursue what truly brings you joy? Not someday, but now, through small, honest ways.

3. What is one thing you could do just for yourself?
   - each day
   - each week
   - each month
   - each year

4. Where could you create space for small joys in your everyday life? What moments already exist that you could savor instead of rushing past?

Integration

How might easing, evaluating, and enjoying help restore balance in your life? What would feel different if joy was treated as essential, not optional?

PART THREE

When the Quicksand Returns

CHAPTER 9

Returning to Solid Ground

I remember the exact day I re-entered quicksand: June 22, 2023. I walked into a client's office with to-go salads for a meeting scheduled during the lunch hour. When my client asked how my day was going, I said, "I have had a great day! I did Pilates and got my hair cut this morning, and now I have meetings with my favorite client for the rest of the day. So it's been pretty perfect."

When I tell you my phone rang at that same moment, I need you to hear me. I said, "It's been pretty perfect," and my phone rang. It was my sister, who never calls. She might text me, "Come in, Beanie," which means "Call me when you get a place where you can finish a sentence," but she never calls me. And here she was, calling. I apologized to my client and fired off a quick "call you back after this meeting" text, which was met with another text: "Call me."

That phone call marked the start of a two-plus-year whirlwind with my dad's health. When my sister called that day, he was in excruciating pain that required an ambulance ride to the hospital. The doctors eventually determined that he had a life-threatening blood infection. We almost lost him on the second day of his hospitalization, but he pulled through and started a journey of hospital/rehab/home/repeat that went on for four months. Since then, he's been hospitalized more times than we can count. After two years of this, we became pretty good at juggling it all while caring for him. But in those early months, it was all uncharted territory, and my sister and I were very involved in his care.

Three months to the day after that phone call, I was neck-deep in the quicksand. I was on the heels of another one of my dad's hospitalizations and related late-night hospital visits, calls with his care team, and errand runs. I had three speaking engagements in three cities over three days (good things come in threes, right?). I was an in-demand speaker on burnout and boundaries (oh, the irony), and my business was thriving. It was everything I had dreamed of for my brand-new little business. People were seeking me out to speak and train across the region, and my dance card was full. My kids described my new job as "driving around and talking to people."

The only problem was that I had been losing my voice for a few weeks, and that day, my voice was nowhere to be found. During my 700 miles of driving over two and a half days, my husband said enough was enough. I needed to cancel something. I croaked out a compromise: I would go straight to urgent care for a shot and antibiotics to get my voice and energy back. I think the only reason he didn't argue was so I wouldn't have to keep trying to talk.

I still went to the training the next day, taking my own electric tea kettle with me so I could nurse my voice with hot tea on demand, no matter what the training facility had in their breakroom. (By now, you have realized that I am a little extra, right?) When I finally made it home and could collapse in my bed, I realized I was right back to where I had been in the corporate world: running on the memory of fumes and saying yes to everyone but myself.

The biggest difference was that I didn't have that corporate salary, someone to cover for me while I took time off, or the security that my job would be waiting for me when I returned. The trade-off was supposed to be the flexibility to do what worked for my family, for me, and for my schedule. Yet here I was, burning the candle at both ends and in the middle.

That day was truly a wake-up call. I was completely drained and running on fumes. Accepting every opportunity that came my way meant I had no margin to take care of myself. I questioned whether I had what it took to be a consultant because I felt I was failing. I was completely overwhelmed until I realized I needed to go back to basics to get myself out of the quicksand.

The embarrassing thing is that I was still going onstage, talking about burnout all over town. I was telling my story of how I got out of burnout while I was burning out in real-time. I also operated on the assumption that the previous work I had done to get out of the quicksand meant I would stay out forever. I wouldn't call it naivety; I think it was just the fact that I had worked so hard to get out that I thought I had done all the work needed to stay out for good.

I knew better, but it took going back into the quicksand to realize that it will always be there. The difference now is that I know what I need to do to get out before I sink in completely. In order to extract myself from this new quicksand, I needed to lean on what I learned when I found my way out the first time.

That meant I needed to practice my ABCs. I needed to sleep, take my medicine, drink water, eat food that came from the ground, move my body, and make time for myself. It was going to require asking for help and saying "no" to some things. I understood that I couldn't lose myself in the work of caregiving, and that meant rebuilding a solid foundation.

And so I did exactly that. I slept. I asked my husband to take over the kids for a weekend morning so I could sleep late. When I finally emerged, I filled my giant cup with water, grabbed some blankets, and cuddled up to my kids on the couch. I kept my phone on the charger to eliminate mindless scrolling. We made sure dinner that night was healthy and served earlier than normal to get me to bed at a reasonable hour. I declined any other obligations, left texts unread, and gave myself permission to disconnect from other distractions. I called my dad before I went to bed to check on him and make plans to see him the next day so that my mind could rest.

The next day, I took the early shift at the hospital, arriving in time for his doctor's rounds. I visited with my dad's care team, made sure he had everything he needed, and tidied up his room. I stayed as long as I could, but I had a car repair appointment that couldn't be put off any longer.

When my husband met me at the mechanic, I must have looked as tired as I felt. He said, "I bet you are ready for a nap now." I replied, "Actually, I think I am just in time to make it to the noon Pilates class." He looked at me like I was crazy, but I understood that what I needed more than sleep was to stretch, breathe, and move my body.

After an hour-long class, my husband came to pick me up for a second time that day. This time, I was re-energized and ready to relieve the sitter so I could spend time with my kids, niece, and nephew. I had trusted myself enough to know what I needed, and I felt reenergized as a result.

That understanding of what I needed and how to refill my cup was new to me, but continuing to apply what I had learned meant I stayed aboveground. If it sounds simple, it is. Once you know what keeps your head out of the quicksand, you just have to keep doing it, even when it feels impossible or selfish.

You don't need to carry everything with you as you move forward. You only need to remember this: **quicksand is not the end of the story. It's a signal. And now, you know how to respond.**

Returning to solid ground is not about avoiding hard seasons. It's about trusting yourself to recognize them, meet them with compassion, and find your footing again, as many times as you need.

SOLID GROUND

Returning to Solid Ground (Again & Again)

1. Where do you see signs of quicksand in your life right now, if any? What feels heavier, murkier, or more difficult than it needs to be?

2. How quickly do you usually notice those signs? What helps you recognize when something is wrong in your body, relationships, or inner dialogue?

3. What do you tend to lean on when things feel hard: Authenticity, Boundaries, or Counterbalance? Which one feels within reach right now?

4. What would it look like to return to your ABCs without waiting for things to get worse? Where could awareness, a boundary, or a small act of counterbalance help you find a steadier footing?

5. What has this journey taught you about your capacity to recover? How has your understanding of burnout, resilience, or yourself shifted?

SOLID GROUND

The ABC Reset

When something feels off, like when you're tired, irritable, disconnected, or doubting yourself, revisit these three questions. This can take five to fifteen minutes. You can do it in your head, on paper, or during a quiet moment alone.

A: Authenticity

- What am I ignoring or overriding in myself right now?
- What do I know to be true that I haven't been honoring about my values, energy, needs, or limits?

B: Boundaries

- What needs to be protected, paused, or renegotiated?
- Where am I giving too much, especially to expectations I never agreed to?

C: Counterbalance

- What could help restore balance, even a little?
- What would ease, evaluate, or bring a small moment of joy back to this season?

Making the ABCs Sustainable

The ABCs work best when they're woven into real life, not saved for emergencies.

You might return to them:

- at the end of a hard week
- during a seasonal transition
- when your body sends an early warning signal
- after you notice resentment, exhaustion, or self-doubt creeping in

Trust the practice. You won't always feel better right away. What you will feel is more centered, more like yourself. That's how you know you're back on solid ground. Life will keep happening. The difference now is that you don't have to disappear inside it. You know how to return to yourself, your values, and the life you're building.

CHAPTER 10

Into the Sunlight

My first boss taught me that experience isn't the best teacher; it is the *only* teacher. While that is absolutely true, I hope you can learn from my experience and cut down the time it takes for you to realize you're sinking.

It is easy to slip back into the old patterns that found me in the bathroom that January night. Probably for you too. So many messages we receive every day tell us to do more, to keep pushing even when we are drowning. Being a solopreneur increases the risk of falling into the trap of overworking, overperforming, and overwhelming yourself. Now that I know just how much I don't want to go back to that quicksand, I am better at catching myself when I see old habits re-emerging. Each time I remember what I have learned along the way, it reinforces that I am on the right path.

Recovering from burnout is not linear. Life doesn't stop just because you found your patch of solid ground. People will get sick, work will be busy, and spirit week will come every May, whether you have the time for it or not. The quicksand doesn't mean you have failed; it means you are human. You can't help falling in again, but you can change how quickly you get out when you do.

I don't always get it right. I still run myself down when my husband travels or during a busy season at work. Workouts get shuffled to take my parents to appointments, and drive-thru meals happen more often some weeks than others. The difference now is I can recognize when I am approaching quicksand, and I know how to change course.

Authenticity has taught me to be mindful of the rhythms of my days and the school year and to protect my calendar from myself and others. I make decisions about everything: my schedule, my attire, my hair, that bring me joy and confidence. The boundaries I keep with myself are probably the most important, and they help me care a little less every day about what other people think of me and prioritize my joy. I look for big and small ways to balance seasons of hustle with time to pause, rather than pushing endlessly.

I have finally realized there is more to life than seeing how high you can climb and how fast you can get there. As it turns out, I was never climbing for myself after all. It was all to meet some imaginary, meaningless expectation.

The only thing that really matters is living a life worth remembering. Embrace the unique and quirky qualities that make you who you are and live your life out loud. Throw your head back and laugh without abandon at a joke you just cracked. Sing a song at the top of your lungs, not worrying about who might hear. Walk away from a sink full of dishes to watch the sunset. Find pride in a workout, a nap, or a crossword puzzle. Plant your feet on solid ground and realize it looks a little different than you imagined, but this new territory is yours and yours alone.

When I lost my brother, I promised myself that I would live a life that he would be proud to watch unfold. It took me a while, but I feel like I get a little closer every day. I caught a glimpse of myself in the mirror the other day, wild-haired, makeup-free, with an ear-to-ear grin, laughing at an inside joke with my kids. It was a version of me I hadn't seen in a long time, and I am working every day to welcome her with open arms. She was a version of me that I know my brother would recognize.

Sharing my story has taken me a long time, and I am grateful to everyone who encouraged me to keep going, and to each of you for reading this book. I hope it helps you find your favorite version of yourself, cheering on others from a patch of solid ground in the sunlight.

ACKNOWLEDGEMENTS

This book was a multi-year labor of love that came together with the help of family, friends, and an amazing team of women who helped me get it across the finish line. I cannot possibly acknowledge everyone who loves me so well, because my village is big and beautiful. From my family (by blood, by marriage or by choice) to my group chat besties, my lifelong friends to my neighbors and former coworkers, just know that I adore you and I am grateful for you.

For Brad, the one who has loved me through every season and is always waiting with fizzy water and a ladder to bring me out of the quicksand. Thank you for believing in me and for holding down the fort every time I disappear to write. I am the luckiest (and it's in a book now, so I win).

To Porter, my incredible and brilliant boy, watching you become the most authentic version of yourself has been an absolute delight. Thank you for inspiring me to do the same (right down to our twin hair!) and for being the best sounding board a mom could ask for.

Vivian, my bold and beautiful girl, your grasp of boundaries and your ability to uphold them may be what ensures you take over the world, and I can't wait to watch. Sorry about that flipped stroller, and thanks for letting me tell that story over and over again.

For my darling parents, for being my biggest cheerleaders and always believing in me. Thank you for surrounding me with books, magazines, encyclopedias, and spirited debate, instilling in me a love of language and the courage to share my voice.

Sisterbestfriend, thank you for loving me fiercely and also calling me out on my BS when I need it (which is often). I am so inspired by your writing and your ability to articulate your grief during this season. I love you more than my luggage!

Sally, this book would still be in a Google Drive folder with 42 different file names if it weren't for you. Thank you for your time, talent, and tenacity in making this a reality. I will be forever grateful for your belief in me and for your willingness to read and re-read every single iteration.

Brigette, your big ideas and thoughtful approach to writing and telling people I was writing changed the course of this story, and I am so grateful.

Jen, thank you for my beautiful cover and for fitting my big ideas onto the pages. You helped make the book reflect my journey both inside and out.

Thanks to Mikaela and her team for transforming a Frankenbook into a real book!

To everyone who responded to my survey and shared their story, thank you for your vulnerability and willingness to help others on their journey out of the quicksand. You helped me feel less alone and reassured me that I was on the right path.

Finally, thank you to everyone who picked up this book. Whether you simply cracked the spine or read it all the way to the end, it means the world to me that you are here!

BIBLIOGRAPHY

1. Engber, Daniel. "Terra Infirma." *Slate*, August 10, 2010. https://www.slate.com/articles/health_and_science/science/2010/08/terra_infirma.html.

2. Mulaney, John. *New in Town*. Comedy album. New York: Comedy Central Records, 2012. ("Quicksand.")

3. *The Croods: Family Tree*. Universal City, CA: DreamWorks Animation, 2021. Television series.

4. World Health Organization. (2019). Burn-out an "occupational phenomenon": International Classification of Diseases. https://www.who.int

5. Mutschler, Phyllis. 2015. "Women and Caregiving: Facts and Figures." Family Caregiver Alliance. 2015. https://www.caregiver.org/resource/women-and-caregiving-facts-and-figures/.

6. "How the Mental Load Affects U.S. Women: The Unsustainable Pressure of Caregiving." 2019. New America. 2019. https://www.newamerica.org/the-thread/sustainable-caregiving-us-women-mental-load/.

7. Maslach, Christina, and Michael P. Leiter. 2016. "Understanding the Burnout Experience: Recent Research and Its Implications for Psychiatry." *World Psychiatry* 15 (2): 103–11. https://doi.org/10.1002/wps.20311.

8. Nagoski, Emily, and Amelia Nagoski. *Burnout: The Secret to Unlocking the Stress Cycle*. New York: Ballantine Books, 2019.

9. Urban, Melissa. *The Book of Boundaries: Set the Limits That Will Set You Free*. New York: Dial Press Trade Paperback, 2022.

If this resonated, don't let it end here.

Scan the code to get practical tools, stay connected, and take your next step out of the quicksand.

www.ingramcontent.com/pod-product-compliance
Lightning Source LLC
LaVergne TN
LVHW090528110826
845146LV00003B/1026

* 9 7 9 8 2 3 4 0 2 9 3 6 2 *